BABY
ANIMALS

BABY
ANIMALS

DEREK HALL

FALL
RIVER
PRESS

This 2009 edition
published by Fall River Press by arrangement
with Regency House Publishing Limited

Fall River Press
122 Fifth Avenue
New York, NY 10011

ISBN: 978-1-4351-0728-1

1 3 5 7 9 10 8 6 4 2

Printed in Singapore

CONTENTS

INTRODUCTION 6

INTRODUCTION

Human beings find animal babies enduringly appealing, for the young of many of these species are often prettier, softer, and more helpless than their parents, stimulating in us an instinct to protect what is small and vulnerable. Even animals that would be dangerous to us when fully grown, as babies they are perceived to be non-threatening and 'safe.' Little wonder, therefore, that young animals should feature so heavily in picture books, calendars, and should be guaranteed to tug at our heart strings in movies and cartoons. Here, we discover not only what is so attractive about these small creatures, but also some of the fascinating ways in which animals, once they have become fully grown, are able to give birth to their own young, then care for them during one of the most vulnerable and momentous periods of their young lives.

All living things must reproduce in order to ensure the continuation of the species. In simple organisms, this may simply involve splitting themselves in half or into fragments, when the pieces will form new individuals. At the other end of the scale, higher animals, such as the great apes and, of course, human beings themselves, invest many years in the process of gestating, protecting and rearing their young. Some animals, such as elephants and whales, produce only a single offspring at each mating, and may not breed again

RIGHT: A giant panda mother with cub.

OPPOSITE: An emperor penguin family with its single chick.

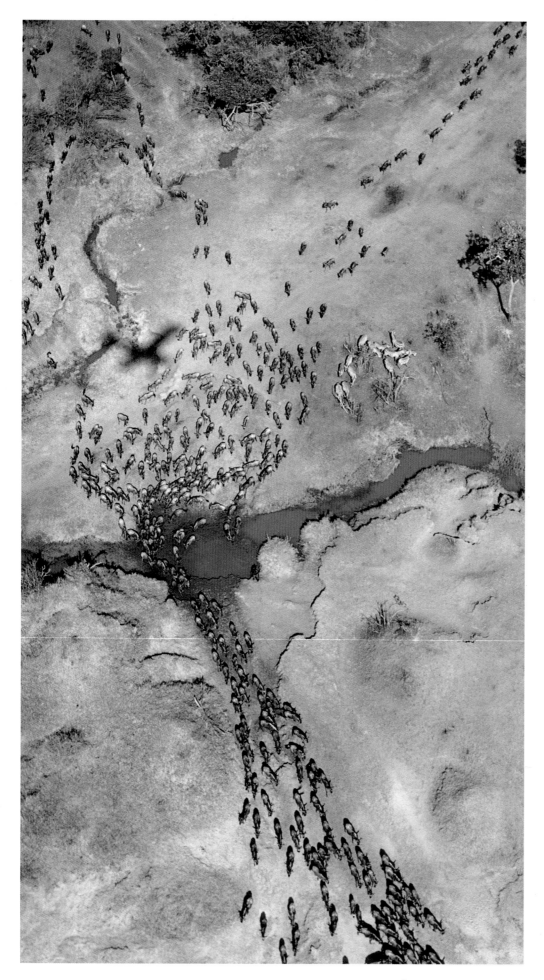

for several years, making the need to protect such a precious individual of even greater importance. In other animals, such as fish and many of the lower species, breeding consists simply of producing thousands, or even millions, of eggs and scattering them in the water. Many, perhaps most, of these eggs will be eaten by other animals, but enough will survive to hatch into young in sufficient numbers to ensure the species will continue. Even then, the chances of survival without any form of parental protection are slim, and many will fall victim to predators. But enough will escape to grow to adulthood and will themselves eventually breed, thus repeating the hazardous but fascinating cycle all over again.

SPREADING OUT

The process of breeding is inextricably linked with dispersal. For a species to be successful, the offspring need to spread and colonize new areas and occupy new territories, otherwise, they would simply be competing for the same resources as their parents. For many marine animals, the ocean environment is a ready-made dispersal mechanism. In the life cycle of a great variety of fish and other marine species, the larval stage is spent floating in the water as part of the plankton – the vast swarm of minute creatures that drift more or less at the mercy of the relentless tides and currents, and which form a vital link in the food chain of marine life. After a time

LEFT: An aerial view of migrating wildebeest.

OPPOSITE ABOVE: A male frigatebird, puffing out his red pouch to attract a mate.

OPPOSITE BELOW: A pair of courting Siberian tigers.

bird will often bring tempting food offerings to his prospective 'bride' as a way of convincing her that he will provide food for a prospective family. Even before that, much display and territorial and mating battles may be necessary before a male gets the chance to impregnate his partner.

MAKING A NEST

Think of a safe, cozy place where babies can be reared and a bird's nest comes immediately to mind, for birds are the master-builders of the animal kingdom. From the simple scrape on the ground, utilized by grouse and many other ground-nesting species, to the elaborate, hanging communal structures, built by sociable weavers, nest-building is the most obvious sign that the breeding season is under way.

spent drifting in the plankton, the larvae develop into small adults, but by now carried far from the places in which they were born. Other animals move away from their parental range once they are weaned, driven away by their parents or by the instinctive desire to establish territories of their own.

ATTRACTING A MATE

Before the process of birth and the rearing of the young can begin, animals must first find mates and copulate with them, an activity that is almost as varied as the animals themselves. Every type of encounter is to be found, from animals that pair for life and those that pair for a season or only for a single mating, to those that aim to reproduce with as many partners as possible. Many animals perform elaborate rituals and procedures before mating; this may be not only to establish and cement the pair bond, but also prove to the female that the male suitor is fit and able enough to perform the task of fatherhood. A male

Many birds' nests are easy to spot, indeed it would be difficult to miss those of rooks or gannets, for example. But other nests are well hidden from view by foliage or built inside hollowed out trees. Despite popular belief, birds do not live in their nests all year round; they use them only when laying eggs and rearing their young, being places where the young can be kept warm, protected, and well-fed.

OPPOSITE: A lesser masked weaver hanging from its nest.

ABOVE: A black-browed albatross in the Falklands, its nest re-used from year to year.

RIGHT: The nest of an American coot.

within range. Some members of the Cichlidae, a major family of perciform fish, attach their eggs to the insides of crevices and underwater caves, using such places as temporary nest sites.

Among the reptilians, estuarine crocodiles and American alligators also build nests, constructing huge piled up mounds made from sticks, mud and vegetation, measuring up to 10ft (3m) across and 39in (1m) high. They then bury their eggs inside their mounds, often sitting on top of them to keep guard. As the vegetation rots in the hot sun, it will give off heat, helping to incubate the eggs – a strategy also adopted by birds such as the mallee fowl of Australia. Other reptilian nests, like those of sea turtles, are simply holes dug in the sand by the female before she deposits her eggs, which are then left to hatch alone.

For some mammals, however, nest-building is not a viable option, and animals such as elephants, for example, may be simply too big to conceal in nests, while others, such as whales, may inhabit an environment where nesting is impossible. Many mammals, however, do build nests for their young, ranging, in the case of woodland species such as deer, from simple grassy areas hidden deep among bracken and other vegetation, to the special nesting chambers in underground tunnel systems built by badgers.

The parents may go to elaborate lengths to keep predators from their nests, some feigning injury by flapping and hopping away from the nest site with drooping wings, hoping to fool a predator into following them. Once a safe distance from the nest, the bird then flies away, by which time the predator has hopefully forgotten its reason for being there. Rabbits are among the animals that conceal the nest entrance whenever they leave, and many

Nest-building is not solely the domain of birds, however. A great many animals build such havens for their young, one being the stickleback, a small freshwater fish. During the breeding season the male builds an arched structure using waterweeds, into which he entices several females to lay their eggs. After fertilizing the eggs, the male stands guard over his brood, fanning water over the eggs to oxygenate them and fiercely seeing off potential predators and others that come

OPPOSITE: Tadpoles feeding on waterweed.

RIGHT: Young ducklings foraging for food.

BELOW: This young fawn, well-camouflaged against leaves, is lying still and quiet to avoid attracting attention until its mother's return.

animals only visit the nest when they need to suckle and care for the young; at other times they stay away, hoping this will prevent predators from being alerted to the whereabouts of the nest.

The young often play their own part in keeping safe: chicks usually remain silent when their parents are absent, cheeping and opening their gaping mouths only when they return with food. Fawns will also lie

motionless on the woodland floor when left alone, while the coloration of these and other animals also helps them to remain concealed. Some juvenile fish have quite different coloration from the adults, which may prevent other adult fish from viewing them as rivals, and thus prevent them from being attacked.

CARE OF THE YOUNG

For those species that undertake a degree of parental care, there is much to be done once the young are born. The young may need regular feeding, and for those species whose young are born relatively helpless, they may need help and stimulation in defecating as well. In addition to these

BELOW: A mother brown bear suckling her cubs.

OPPOSITE: A young rabbit feeding on herbage.

chores, the parent or parents must maintain a high level of protection of their offspring, finding food for themselves and more often for their young. In some species the male assists in these tasks, but in many others the task is left to the female alone. Once the young have reached a certain stage in their development they may need to be taught the social and hunting skills that will equip them for a life on their own or as part of a hierarchical group or pack. Elephants and meerkats are among the diverse group of animals that share the task of rearing juveniles – tasks that are usually carried out by older siblings, giving the mother a welcome break.

Some animals never leave the family group: for example, female elephants remain with their mother's herd and become part of a roaming herd that may comprise 100 or more individuals. Males, however, leave their mothers once they are mature, forming bachelor groups and leaving them only when strong enough to challenge the dominant bull of another herd.

All over the world, therefore, on countless occasions, millions upon millions

OPPOSITE: An Atlantic puffin, its beak festooned with sand eels, which it has caught to feed its chick.

BELOW: A Japanese macaque baby clings to its mother.

of animals, of each and every species, react to blind instinct, something they cannot possibly understand, and embark upon the most important act in nature – the drama of creating new life, leading to the most precarious and fascinating stage of all – the birth of an animal baby.

CHAPTER ONE
FARM ANIMALS & PETS

DOMESTIC CHICKEN
(*Gallus gallus domesticus*)

Domestic chickens have been with us for over 2,000 years, and there is hardly a place in the world that does not rely on them as a source of meat and eggs.

The chicken is even prized as a pet bird, and there has been plenty of scope to develop exotic and ornamental varieties for showing and keeping. Its nearest ancestor is thought to be the red jungle fowl, one of the four species of wild Asian jungle fowl that inhabit India and South-East Asia.

Chickens are usually ready to breed at about 18 to 24 weeks. As in other birds, the egg is coated with a hard, waterproof shell as it travels down the lower part of the hen's oviduct. Domestic hens may lay their eggs in a scrape in the ground if no other nesting site is available, but many hens kept in hen houses and coops lay their eggs in specially prepared nesting boxes. Incubation lasts for approximately 21 days, the chicks emitting cheeping sounds when they are ready to hatch; the hen then encourages them to peck their way out of their shells by gently clucking to them.

Baby chickens are covered in fluffy down feathers, and have tiny unfeathered wings. They are very appealing. Depending on the breed, they may be brown, cream or a mixture of these or other colors. The hen occasionally feeds the chicks, but more often simply calls them toward any sources of food or water she may have found. She also puts a protective wing around them when they are small, but after a few weeks begins to lose interest in her growing brood and they are gradually left to fend for themselves.

The egg is widely seen as a symbol of life, just as a new life emerges from an egg when the chick hatches out. Specially decorated eggs are given to celebrate Easter or the beginning of spring, the oldest tradition being to use dyed or painted chicken eggs; but chocolate eggs are used in modern times, supposedly hidden by the Easter Bunny for good children to find on Easter Day.

DOMESTIC DUCK (*Anas* species)

Ducks are popular pets, also valuable farm animals, reared mainly for their tasty meat, eggs and down. Many domestic ducks are descendants of commonly occurring wild species, such as the mallard (*Anas platyrhynchos*). Ducks tend to be easier to rear than chickens, since they are generally hardier and less prone to disease.

BABY ANIMALS

In the most natural of conditions, ducks may have free access to ponds and quiet secluded places in which to build a nest, although the prevalence of cats and foxes means that a more secure shelter is usually offered.

Nests are built on the ground and are constructed of grasses lined with feathers, in which between nine and 13 grey-green eggs are incubated by the female for about 26 days. The fluffy duck chicks are well-developed when they are hatched, and will immediately follow their mother to the safety of water after their feathers have dried. Here they will plunge in, then bob to the surface, readying themselves for swimming and to begin feeding on insects. They follow their mother everywhere until they are big enough to fend for themselves. Fledging takes between 50 and 60 days.

Domesticated ducks can be kept as pets in gardens or backyards where there are ponds, although they will probably gobble up all the wildlife and frogspawn, and even swallow adult frogs and toads. Because their size hinders them from flying properly, a coop should be provided to shelter them from predators, such as cats, foxes, hawks, coyotes, and racoons.

HORSE (*Equus caballus*)

Some of the best-known horse breeds include the heavy draft varieties, such as the Shire and Percheron, and the riding types, such as the Andalusian and Hanoverian. In the wild, horses give birth without intervention or assistance from human beings, but horses kept in domestic circumstances are usually provided with a quiet, safe place such as a loose box, where they can give birth in comfort. Behavior before mating, however, is the same for both wild and domestic horses. The female (mare) advertises her readiness to mate by urinating and raising her tail. The male (stallion) approaches and nuzzles her to determine her readiness, and if all seems in order he will mount her.

The mare will carry her young, or foal, for 11 months. Usually, single foals are born, although occasionally the mare produces twins. Birth takes place in the spring, generally at night or early in the morning. (In the wild, this may be a strategy designed to reduce the likelihood of predators spotting the newborn animal.) As soon as the foal is born, the mother will chew away the placental membranes to prevent the foal from suffocating. She then gently nuzzles it, licking it dry and stimulating its circulation. Soon the foal will attempt to feed on its mother's milk, and within an hour or so will also try to stand. It may take three or four attempts before the foal's spindly, wobbly legs can get it to its feet, raising itself on its hind legs first before its front legs. The foal will

Horse breeds are loosely divided into three categories based on general temperament: spirited hotbloods, that possess speed and endurance; coldbloods, such as draft horses and some ponies, that are suitable for slow, heavy work; and warmbloods, that were developed from crosses between the first two categories, to create horses to be used in specific riding tasks.

suckle from its mother for up to six months, although as its teeth start to grow it will also begin to nibble at grass. For the next few months the foal grows steadily and begins to explore its surroundings, although it stays close to its mother's side. For her part, she is an attentive and protective parent.

PONY

Ponies are small horses, and in many ways share the same basic anatomy, behavior and requirements as horses, although some breeds of pony are especially hardy, two of the best-known being the Shetland and the Connemara. Being smaller animals, the foals of ponies are smaller than those of horses, but they are both born in a similar way. Like horse foals, pony foals have disproportionately long legs compared with the rest of their bodies, although this imbalance disappears as they grow. Again like horse foals, pony foals can focus their eyes shortly after they are born, and do not cut all their milk teeth until they are about six months old. The young pony is considered fully grown at four years old.

DONKEY

(*Equus asinus* or *Equus africanus*)

The smallest member of the Equidae or horse family, the donkey's ancestor is the African wild ass, that was first domesticated in North Africa about 6,000 years ago. It is found the world over, where it is frequently used in the service of mankind, having been used as a beast of burden for thousands of years; but there are also feral populations in Australia and parts of North and South America. It is an extremely hardy creature that can exist on poor grazing and that will tolerate quite hot, arid conditions. It is also friendly, calm and endearing, often kept as a pet. It can live for as long as 50 years.

It was prophesied that the Messiah would arrive riding on a donkey which, in the context of the Hebrew Bible, suggests it was a mount befitting such an iconic figure, at a time when commoners went on foot. Later, however, the idea of Jesus, the Christian Messiah, riding a donkey into Jerusalem, came to have a different meaning, indicating a simplicity and humility that was emulated by saints such as Francis of Assisi.

Donkeys have an average gestation period of 12 months. Twins are rare, as in horses, although they are slightly more common in donkeys. The birth process, aftercare and development of the donkey foal is similar to that of the horse.

SHEEP (*Ovis aries*)

There are about 300 different breeds and varieties of sheep, and they are found worldwide, except in extremely cold climates. Sheep were first domesticated in the region that includes the modern-day states of Israel, Syria, Lebanon, Turkey and Iraq, about 10,000 years ago. There are estimated to be well over 100 million sheep throughout the world, with the largest concentration in Australia. Although most sheep are kept as domestic stock, mainly for their wool and meat, there are also feral populations, as well as wild sheep known as mouflon. Merinos, Sudanese, Corriedales and blackface are just a few of the many breeds available.

Normally a flock of ewes (females) is mated by a single ram (male). Most sheep breed seasonally, but some breed all year round. Most lambs are born in the spring after a pregnancy of 143 to 159 days, with the ewe giving birth to either one or two offspring. On average, lambs weigh about 9lbs (4kg) at birth. Lambs are born fully developed and are able to run around only a few hours after leaving their mother's womb. At birth, lambs have long tails, but these are often shortened by the farmer to

Sheep have a unique place in human culture, most often associated with the pastoral idea of the ideal Arcadian landscape, and figuring in many mythologies. It is important in religious ritual, used in sacrifice and associated with Christ, the Lamb of God.

prevent them from becoming entangled in bushes and with wire fencing once they begin to roam. Once the lamb is born, it needs to bond with its mother, and both must learn to recognize each other's sound and smell before they rejoin the flock. Once bonded, a mother ewe will allow no other lamb but her own to suckle. Sheep's milk is richer in fat and protein than cow's milk, and the lamb suckles for about four months before turning its attention to grass and other vegetation.

GOAT (*Capra hircus aegagrus*)

There are over 200 breeds of goat, including the Anglo-Nubian, the Nordic, the Angora, and the Toggenberg. Most goats are found in warm and temperate countries, where they are kept in huge numbers, especially in dry, scrubby regions, for they are able to exist on a diet of sparse, even thorny, vegetation. Their feeding habits, however, have caused concern in some regions, such as on the border of the southern Sahara Desert, where they have denuded the already sparse and fragile vegetation, thus increasing the

spread of desertification. Being so nimble, they are also able to climb trees, getting at vegetation that other types of browsing ruminants cannot reach. Goats have been herded for at least 9,000 years, and in addition to the domestic types, feral and wild goats also exist in parts of the world. Goats are mainly kept for their meat, but their hides and milk are also prized, and in some regions – such as Nepal – they are also used as pack animals.

Goats become sexually mature at four to six months of age, and mating occurs between September and March. The gestation period is 150 days, after which time the female (known as the nanny or doe) gives birth to one to three offspring, known as kids. Weaning takes about ten to 12 weeks, although the kids start to take solid food from two to three weeks of age to help the development of the rumen (a special part of the stomach that is involved

with the digestion of their food). Young goats are inquisitive and lively animals, and soon develop a 'pecking-order' hierarchy among themselves. Being agile climbers, the young kids are soon clambering about on anything they can find – including their mother!

Goats have horizontal, slit-shaped pupils, an adaptation which increases peripheral vision.

PIG (*Sus domestica*)

The domestic pig is a much misunderstood animal; regarded chiefly as nothing more than a valuable source of food, it is in fact an intelligent creature, often proving to be easier to train than a dog. In recent times, some breeds, such as the Vietnamese pot-bellied pig, have been kept as pets. About 800 million pigs are kept worldwide, almost half of which are found in Asia alone. Pig meat is used in many different ways, and the skin, fat and bristles are utilized as well. In the Perigord region of France, pigs are trained to sniff out valuable truffles (a kind of edible fungus), using their sensitive snouts, while in some places they are kept by families for their own use, and are allowed to roam freely, eating roots, worms and food scraps. In other places they are farmed, either in small operations or in large, intensive systems. Popular pig breeds include the Tamworth, landrace, saddleback, duroc and Andalusian.

In tropical countries, breeding can occur throughout the year, peaking in the rainy seasons. Female pigs can conceive at about eight months of age, with pregnancy lasting for about 115 days. Females are known as gilts before they have mated, and as sows afterwards. Litters can range from about six to 16 piglets, but even bigger litters have been known. The piglets are suckled by the sow for about three weeks; to do this, she will lie on her side, with the hungry and eager piglets jostling to get access to a teat. After weaning, the piglets start to eat solid foods.

Despite the pig's reputation for gluttony and dirtiness, a lesser known but more important quality is their lively intelligence.

COW (*Bos* species)

Cows (females) and bulls (males) belong to the group of ruminant (cud-chewing) animals known as cattle, of which there are about 200 different species, kept worldwide as sources of milk, meat and leather. In some places, such as Africa and Asia, cattle are also used as draft animals. Cattle were first domesticated about 9,000 years ago. One-sixth of all the world's cattle are to be found in India. Most cattle are bred either for their milk (dairy cattle) or for their meat (beef cattle). Well-known dairy cows include the Friesian, Jersey and dairy shorthorn. Popular beef cattle include the Texas longhorn, the Hereford, and the Charolais. In parts of Australia and the American West, the cattle are grazed on huge ranches numbering tens of thousands of animals, while elsewhere they may be reared in pastures on small farms.

Most females are about two years old when they have their first calf, before which they are known as heifers. Pregnancy lasts for about 283 days, and nearly always only a single calf is born. The calf feeds on its mother's rich milk until it is between eight and nine weeks old. As well as providing nourishment, the mother's milk provides

Cattle are ruminants, in that they have a digestive system that allows otherwise indigestible foods to be digested by repeatedly regurgitating and rechewing them as 'cud.' This is then reswallowed and further digested by specialized micro-organisms in the rumen, that are responsible for decomposing cellulose and other carbohydrates into volatile fatty acids that are their primary metabolic fuel.

the developing calf with vital antibodies that protect it from disease. Calves are born with small horns, which are often removed by a vet.

DOG (*Canis familiaris*)

The domestic dog has been both a friend and a valuable working animal in the service of humankind for thousands of years. Tough, intelligent and able to be bred and trained to perform a wide variety of tasks, the dog serves us in ways ranging from guard dog, guide dog and livestock herder to retriever, sniffer dog and pack animal. The dog is descended from the wolf, although the exact lineage, and even the way in which domestication came about, is open to some conjecture. Suffice to say that over thousands of years an inseparable and unique bond has been forged between the dog and its many human admirers, and dogs were known to the ancient Egyptians thousands of years ago. Today's breeds of dog are often classified according to their general shape or the kind of work they perform. Thus there are hounds, gundogs, terriers, general-purpose or utility dogs, working dogs and toy (small breed) dogs.

Among the animals kept as pets, arguably none is more endearing, amusing, playful and rewarding than the dog, and this is perhaps especially so when it is a puppy. However, a puppy needs not only its mother's care and attention, but will in time also need firm but understanding care and training from its human owner to ensure that it grows to be a stable and well-behaved animal. A dog that is out of control and untrained is a danger and a nuisance to almost everyone, including itself. The dog is a pack animal by nature, and one of the lessons it must learn is that it has its place in the hierarchical system that includes its human owner as the pack leader or 'top dog.'

In 1993, dogs were reclassified as a subspecies of the gray wolf, Canis lupus, *by the Smithsonian Institution and the American Society of Mammalogists.*

The huge variation in dog types means there is also variation in the age at which the female dog becomes mature enough to breed, but it is normally at between four and 18 months of age. The period during which a female is ready to copulate is known as the 'heat.' Following mating, a pregnancy lasts for between 59 to 65 days, the average being 63 days. The average litter size for the dog is six puppies, but there is much variation here, again often related to the breed in question, with large breeds producing larger litters (in some cases up to 15 pups may be produced in a single litter).

When a female is ready to give birth, she will exhibit changes in her behavior for which the owner should watch. She will appear restless, lose her appetite, and will usually start to prepare a nest in a quiet spot by tearing up paper or similar material. There will also be a drop in her body temperature. At this point she should be provided with a suitable whelping, or birth, box and the owner should ensure that she is not disturbed but is ready to be helped if anything seems to be going wrong with the birth.

Puppies are usually born within about 20 minutes of one another, although the mother may 'take a break' between deliveries, so the whole process may take several hours – even longer on occasions. A vet should be called if the mother is visibly straining but no puppies have been delivered for an hour or so. Puppies are normally born head first, and are encased in membranes and with their umbilical cords attached. The mother bites through

the umbilical cord, releases the puppy from the membrane, and licks it vigorously to stimulate breathing.

Puppies are born blind with very limited mobility and without the ability to defecate or urinate without external stimulation. They can, however, smell, taste and touch, and can also cry to attract their mother's attention. The puppy has an innate ability to suckle, however, and once nudged to one of its mother's teats will begin to feed happily. When they are very young the mother moves the puppies around in the whelping box to assemble

them for feeding or to put them safely to one side so that they can sleep.

The puppy becomes steadily stronger and more mobile, and at about 12 days opens its eyes. Weaning starts at about three weeks, beginning with a milk meal when the mother is out of the whelping box, then meat, cereal and puppy meal is slowly introduced. In due course, the puppy will become more and more independent and will start to explore its surroundings, testing everything it encounters by sniffing and chewing it, and will interact with its siblings.

Once a puppy leaves its mother and comes into the care of its new owner, it must be carefully looked after and properly trained to ensure it has a happy life. Puppy ownership is a big responsibility and should not be taken on unless there is the time and determination to carry it out properly. A happy puppy, however, will more than repay the kindness, patience and care given to it by its owner. Its amusing antics, willingness to play, endearing and affectionate nature, will soon ensure it becomes an important and much-loved member of the human family.

CAT (*Felis catus*)

The domestic cat bears a remarkably close resemblance to its truly wild relatives, such as the African wildcat (*Felis sylvestris lybica*) and the European wildcat (*Felis sylvestris*). Cats were probably first domesticated about 5,000 years ago, and soon earned their keep by catching the rats and other rodents that were the scourge of granaries and other places where food was stored. They are still prized in many places for this function, but today most cats are kept simply as pets, but ironically in this role, their hunting behavior is now frowned upon because of the heavy toll they can take on the garden bird and shrew populations. Over the thousands of years of its association with mankind, the cat has figured hugely in religion, art, myth and folklore, having been raised to the level of a deity in some cultures and to that of a reviled familiar of witches in others. It remains as ever an enigmatic and independent animal, appearing to know much more than it ever lets on! Although most cats are friendly and sociable, they seldom seem to offer the almost unconditional affection and devotion bestowed on us by dogs.

Unlike dogs, which were selectively bred for many different purposes and which resulted in a huge variation in sizes and body shapes, most cat breeding revolves around finding different color mutations, hair types and other fairly subtle body differences. Thus most domestic cats are very similar in build and general appearance. Despite domestication, cats retain most of the traits that make their wild relatives such successful animals. Cats have muscular, flexible bodies and can jump

A skilled predator, the cat is known to hunt over 1,000 species for food. It can be trained to obey simple commands, and individuals have also been known to learn how to manipulate simple mechanisms, such as doorknobs. Cats use body language and vocalizations for different types of communication, which include meowing, purring, hissing, growling, squeaking, chirping, clicking, and grunting.

and climb with ease. The ability of a cat to walk along the top of a fence demonstrates their excellent balancing skills, and some cats, such as the Turkish Van, can even swim. A cat has eyes that enable it to see well at night, and long whiskers that help it feel its way about in very dark conditions. Excellent hearing enables it to locate prey accurately, and the cat's speed of movement ensures that its victim is unlikely to escape.

Domestic cats are classified in several ways, but one of the simplest categorizes them into longhairs, semi-longhairs and shorthairs. Within each of these groups there are many different breeds exhibiting varieties of coat-color and pattern and even hair type. There are also tailless breeds and others with unusual ear-shapes. And in addition to all of these pedigree varieties or breeds there are the many non-pedigree 'moggies,' not to mention new varieties being developed which have yet to achieve classification status. When one considers the fact that although many cats look similar, different breeds have their own individual characters and temperaments, then the choice facing a potential owner is fairly bewildering.

Cats have several periods during the year when they are on 'heat,' or ready to mate, females being ready at four to ten months and males at about six months. The gestation period for cats is 60 to 69 days. The female will need a warm, quiet and

comfortable place to have her kittens, and most owners provide such accommodation, although some cats will often simply find their own spot where they feel safe and secure. Litter sizes usually range from two to eight kittens, but the average is often smaller at about three to five. The kittens are born along with their placentas and with their eyes closed. They are also deaf at birth. The mother bites through the umbilical cords and licks the kittens to stimulate them to make them breathe, then she will encourage them to feed on her milk.

Kittens open their eyes about a week after they are born, and they begin to move around in the nest a week or so after that. For the first few weeks of their life the mother not only feeds them but also keeps them clean. Within a few days they are able to locate her and can wriggle over to her for a feed. They open their eyes at about ten days. By about five weeks of age the kittens will be quite active and keen to explore. The mother will also pick them up gently in her mouth if she wants to bring them back to the nest. They are weaned by the age of six or seven weeks, but by about six weeks they will have begun to take solid food for the first time. Although active by now, kittens should still be kept indoors until weaned to avoid infections, but they should also be provided with a litter tray and be placed on it following a meal; in this way they will eventually learn to be clean about the house.

Kittens are inquisitive, playful animals. Their first months of life are a mixture of frenzied activity interspersed with bouts of deep sleep. At six weeks they will enjoy playing with small toys, such as balls, but should be supervised to ensure they don't injure themselves. They also need supervision at this time to safeguard your curtains, furniture and any precious household items. Training often begins about this time, and owners should reinforce good behavior, such as the kitten coming when you call, and by sharply tapping a table top, or making another sudden noise when naughtiness, such as scratching furniture, persists. In time, a bond should be established with your cat, when it will greet you by nudging its head against you, miaowing to let you know when it needs feeding or wants to go out; it will also seek out your lap when it is time to settle down for a quiet few hours.

GOLDFISH (*Carassius auratus*)

The goldfish was one of the earliest fish to be domesticated, and is still one of the most commonly seen in aquaria and water-gardens. A relatively small member of the carp family, it was first domesticated in China and was introduced to Europe in the late-17th century. Today it is still one of the most popular of all pets, the reasons for this being not very hard to see. It is an inexpensive, hardy, coldwater fish that can live equally happily in an aquarium in the home as in a garden pond. Furthermore, the goldfish is available in a range of colors and with many fin and other body variations, with types including shubunkins, lionheads, veiltails, comets and black moors. Goldfish will eat a variety of foods, including natural items, such as insects, as well as proprietary fish food.

Goldfish breed once a year, usually in late spring. Favored breeding sites are areas of fine-leaved vegetation, and where there are roots in which the female can deposit her eggs; once she has laid them they are fertilized by the male. Many eggs get eaten by other goldfish that may be hovering around, but some usually survive intact. The eggs usually take about a week to hatch, and the young, or fry, carry a yolk sac for the first couple of days, which provides them with their initial nourishment. After that is used up, the young begin to look about for other food.

The oldest recorded goldfish lived 49 years, but most domestic goldfish generally survive only six to eight years, due to being kept confined.

Although highly-regarded, ornamental goldfish, such as orandas, ryukins and ranchus, are often more difficult to maintain, and sell for much higher prices than the more simple varieties.

BUDGERIGAR (*Melopsittacus undulatus*)

The budgerigar is another ever-popular pet, and probably the most commonly kept cagebird. Budgies come in a wide variety of colors, and all are friendly, inquisitive and lively creatures. Budgies have the added attraction of being marvelous mimics, not only of the human voice but also of other sounds they hear repeatedly, such as doorbells and telephones.

Typically, a breeding room is set up containing one or more breeding cages, depending on the number of birds kept. A nest box is wired to the breeding cage so that the birds can easily access it. Once the birds have been paired up, the female is left alone in the breeding cage for a couple of days so that she can become accustomed to both it and her general surroundings; if she is relaxed and feels at home, she is more likely to lay successfully. Next, the male is introduced into the breeding cage so that the pair can mate.

The hen should begin laying in about ten days. The usual clutch size is about four to eight eggs, and it takes 18 days from the first egg being laid to the first chick being

Budgerigars are often referred to as parakeets, in the United States, which is a term for any of a number of small parrots with long, flat tails. The budgerigar is found throughout the drier parts of Australia, where it has survived for the last five million years in the harsh inland conditions of that continent.

hatched. The chicks emerge from the nest box when they are four weeks old, and nearly two weeks later are able to feed for themselves. Their first molt occurs before they are four months old.

LOVEBIRD (*Agapornis* species)

Lovebirds are friendly, colorful and intelligent little birds. One of the smallest members of the parrot family, they are easy to keep and have relatively long lives of up to 20 years. They are sociable birds and do better kept as pairs or in groups. They love to clamber about and learn tricks and are also very vocal, and emit high-pitched screeches to attract their owner's attention! Lovebirds are available in a wide range of different colors, which adds greatly to their appeal.

Lovebirds can be mated from about a year old, and will use a purpose-built nest box or a hollowed-out log of suitable size. They prefer slightly humid conditions, and the nest area should be lined with plenty of damp peat, bark and straw.

The hen begins incubating in earnest after the second or third egg is laid, going on to produce four to six eggs after a 23-day incubation period. Both the male and the female feed the young chicks. The chicks are usually ready to leave the nest at about six weeks, but will return to the nest box at night to share the accommodation

Lovebird is the commonly used name for the genus Agapornis (from the Greek agape, love, and ornis, bird), and can refer to any of the nine species within the group. Eight of these are native to the African continent, while the Madagascar lovebird is indigenous to the island of that name.

with their parents for a further couple of weeks. Once the chicks are feeding independently, breeders usually move the youngsters to another cage so that the parents can breed again.

HAMSTER (includes *Cricetulus, Cricetus, Mesocricetus* and *Phodopus* species)

Hamsters are small rodents which, in the wild, are found from parts of Europe eastward to the Middle East and into Russia and China. The name for these animals comes from the German *hamstern* ('hoarder') and refers to the cheek pouches that all hamsters have and which they stuff with large quantities of food before carrying it back to their burrows for eating later. They continue to exhibit this behavior even when kept in cages as pets, and where there are plentiful supplies of food no more than a few inches from their nests!

Hamsters are popular pets, although by nature they are crepuscular and nocturnal animals – which may explain the nips they sometimes deliver when aroused prematurely from their nests to be played with during the day.

Hamsters become fertile at different ages, depending on the species, but it can be from one to three months, and breeding normally occurs from April to October.

Litter sizes are largest in the Syrian hamster, at eight to ten young, while other hamsters usually produce three to seven in a litter. Gestation is normally 16 to 18 days in the Syrian hamster and 21 days or even longer in other species. Hamsters are hairless and blind at birth, and are born into a nest that the mother has prepared in advance. She lines the nest with leaves in the wild, but pet hamsters are usually offered material such as tissue paper or cotton wool. The young soon begin to explore beyond the nest, and they are completely weaned by 22 or 23 days.

Syrian hamsters are generally solitary and will fight to the death if put together, whereas dwarf hamsters tend to get along with others of the same species. Once a Syrian hamster is tamed it will remain so for a long time.

GUINEA PIG (*Cavia porcellus*)

Guinea pigs get their name from the squeaking, pig-like noises that they make. They make friendly, easy-to-keep and relatively hardy pets, and are thus ideal for children. They can even be housed together with small rabbits, and in fact seem to appreciate the company of other animals. Guinea pigs are members of the Caviidae family, all of which are native to South America, where they are used as food and as a source of fur in some countries. Such is the appeal of the guinea pig, however, that it is now found almost worldwide. Like many other animals kept as domestic pets, the guinea pig is available in a range of colors and different hair types.

The sow (female) is ready to mate at about five months. Boar (male) and sow are simply left together for about six weeks so that mating can occur, after which time the sow should be placed on her own for the duration of her pregnancy, which lasts for 69 days. The young are often born at night, with four being the average litter-size. Baby guinea pigs are capable of nibbling at solid food a few days after birth, but rely on their mother's milk until they are weaned at about 30 days. Within a short time they will be ready to explore outside the nest, accompanied by their ever watchful mother.

Common varieties of guinea pigs found in pet stores are the English or American shorthair, with its short, smooth coat, the Abyssinian, whose coat is ruffled with cowlicks or rosettes, the Peruvian and Sheltie (Silkie), both straight longhair breeds, and the Texel, a curly longhair.

MONGOLIAN GERBIL
(*Meriones unguiculatus*)

Adapted for dry, often hot, environments, gerbils nevertheless make ideal pets. Highly active and amusing to watch, they are likely to become very tame if handled frequently from an early age. There are about 80 different gerbil species found in Africa, the Middle East, and Asia, the most commonly kept as pets being the Mongolian gerbil. These are sociable creatures, that live in burrows when not feeding, and exist on a diet

consisting mainly of seeds. Their front paws are capable of holding food as they are biting into it. The back legs are used to help them jump – something they do extremely well.

Gerbils are ready to breed at about nine weeks of age – even before they are fully grown. It is best to introduce a breeding pair together when they are both very young to reduce the risk of fighting, but if this is not possible then a pair should be introduced on neutral territory. Pregnancy lasts for 24 days, and four to six young are typically born. The babies are helpless and

The Mongolian jird is often confused with Meriones unguiculatus, *but is a separate species, first brought to the US in 1954.*

naked at birth, but start to develop fur on their bodies when about six days old. Their eyes open after a further ten days, and they then begin to move around. The mother picks the babies up in her mouth to carry them from place to place or back to the nest if they stray too far. The young also start to take solid food at about 16 days, although they continue to be weaned until they are 21–25 days old.

CHAPTER TWO
AMPHIBIANS & REPTILES

COMMON FROG (*Rana temporaria*)

This is found in much of Europe (but not in many parts of Spain and Italy) and as far east as Asia. The frog is often found near ponds, streams and marshes, but is actually more or less terrestrial outside the breeding season and may also be encountered in woods, gardens and meadows. Its food is a mixture of slugs, worms and insects. Adults catch their food on land, but young frogs also feed in the water. The long sticky tongue and widely gaping mouth help the frog to quickly catch and then swallow any prey.

Breeding can take place as early as December and as late as March, depending on the weather, but typically takes place in February and March, once the frogs have abandoned their hibernation sites. These include compost heaps, beneath logs, and under the leaves at the bottom of ponds.

For several decades up to the 1970s, the frog had been suffering a serious decline, but it has experienced a welcome recovery since then, due to the increase in popularity of suburban garden ponds, although inbreeding due to this isolation can lead to reduced immunity and an increase in disease.

Males arrive at the breeding sites first and attract females with their rasping croaks.

Mating takes place in the water, and each female lays up to 4,000 eggs at a time, which are fertilized by the male as they are released. The eggs are usually laid in calm, still water, such as typically found in ponds. The eggs, or spawn, are embedded in a gelatinous coating that swells in the water to provide a protective covering for the eggs. The frogspawn floats on the surface, where the sun's rays help to warm the eggs and encourage them to develop.

The larval forms that hatch from the eggs about 30 to 40 days later are known as tadpoles. They have large heads with big eyes, gills for breathing under water, and swimming tails. At first they feed on the jelly-like spawn but quickly move on to algae and other small plants. As the tadpoles grow, they lose their gills and develop lungs and must now take air from the surface to breathe, which is when they start to eat insects as well as algae. Their hind legs develop at about six to nine weeks, and by 11 weeks they have their front legs, too. By about 12 weeks the tails have been absorbed and the tadpoles have turned into miniature froglets. Now they leave the water to hide away in the relative safety of the waterside vegetation. The whole process of development, known as metamorphosis, takes about 14 weeks to complete.

Despite the fact that so many eggs are laid, only about five out of every couple of thousand or so ever develop into adult frogs. Fish, birds, snakes and predatory dragonfly larvae are responsible for most of this heavy toll, and cannibalism between tadpoles also tends to be rife – as anyone who has hatched out frogspawn at home will know!

TREE FROG *(Rhacophoridae, Hylidae)*

Two lineages gave rise to tree frogs, the Rhacophoridae and the Hylidae, both with certain adaptations which predispose them to an arboreal lifestyle. Tree frogs are quite diverse in habit, but spend much of their lives in trees and shrubby vegetation, although some species may choose other lifestyles, depending on environment and inclination. Many millions of years of convergent evolution, resulting in almost identical habitats and ecologies between the two families, have resulted in species that strongly resemble one another. In fact, they are so similar, as regards their ecological niche, that where one group occurs the other is almost always absent. Present-day distribution of these species indicates that the last common ancestor of the two lived long before the extinction of the dinosaurs.

As the name implies, these frogs are typically found in trees or other high-growing vegetation. They do not normally descend to the ground, except for mating, and some even build foam nests on leaves, and rarely leave the trees during their adult lives.

The tree frog's background color is typically a vivid green, uniformly so in some, but subtly patterned in others; this provides excellent camouflage, depending on the particular kind of vegetation inhabited and what predators are to be

Like other amphibians, tree frogs are very sensitive to changes in their natural environment caused by pollution or increased human activity. As a result, some are used as indicators to monitor the environmental health of specific regions of the world.

56

avoided. But many tree frogs can change their color to a remarkable degree, and when resting on bark, for example, they are usually a brownish-gray.

Tree frogs are usually miniscule, as their weight has to be carried by the branches and twigs of their habitat. While some reach 4in (10cm) or more, they are hardly in the same size class as 'grass frogs' (which ironically contain some species belonging to the 'true' tree frogs, Hylidae). Typical in tree frogs are the well-developed discs at the tips of the fingers and toes, and the fingers and toes themselves, as well as the limbs, tend to be rather long, producing superior grasping ability. One genus of the Rhacophoridae is most extreme in this respect, and is able to oppose two fingers to the others, resulting in a vise-like grip.

The Rhacophoridae are the Old World tree frogs (also known as moss frogs) of tropical regions around the Indian Ocean, Africa, South Asia and South-East Asia east to Lydekker's Line, Indonesia, while a few also occur in East Asia. Hylidae, which are the 'true' tree frogs, occur elsewhere – in the temperate to tropical parts of Eurasia, north of the Himalayas, also in Australia and the Americas.

RADIATED TORTOISE
(*Geochelone (Astrochelys) radiata*)

This is one of several species of tortoise found in the warmer parts of the world. Although this species is native only to southern Madagascar, and is mostly only found there, it can also be found in the rest of this country and has been introduced to the islands of Réunion and Mauritius.

The high, domed shell of this tortoise is used, as in other tortoises, as a place in which to retreat when threatened, and the arms, legs and head can all be withdrawn safely into the shell until danger passes. The disadvantage of such a heavy, strong shell is that tortoises can move about only slowly and relatively clumsily as they search for the plants which form their diet. Being herbivores, grazing on grasses produces 80–90 per cent of their diet, while they also eat fruits and succulent plants. They are an endangered species, however, mainly because of the destruction of their habitat by human beings, the fact that they are poached for food, and that they have been over-exploited by the pet trade.

Female radiated tortoises lay between three and 12 eggs in a hole about 6in (15cm) deep, which they have previously dug. Once the eggs are laid they are left to hatch, with incubation taking up to 230 days in this species. On hatching, the whitish baby tortoises are about 1.25in (3.5cm) long, and must quickly scuttle to hide in vegetation to avoid being eaten by predators such as lizards, snakes and birds. Very soon afterwards, the young tortoises develop the domed shell of the adult.

The carapace of this tortoise is brilliantly marked with yellow lines radiating from the center of each dark plate of the shell, hence its name.

NILE CROCODILE
(*Crocodilus niloticus*)

This large crocodile – up to 16.5ft (5m) long – is found in many parts of Africa, where it inhabits large rivers, lakes and marshland. Like other crocodiles, it is highly predatory, often ambushing its prey in the water after drifting imperceptibly within range before mounting a lightning-quick lunge and snatching the victim up in its jaws. Yet despite the reptile's awesome reputation as a hunter, it shows a remarkably gentle side to its nature when it comes to caring for its own young.

After mating, the female lays between 25 and 75 eggs in a special pit she has dug close to the water's edge. The eggs are covered over and then guarded by the female for the three-month incubation period. Once the young have hatched from the eggs, and still secure within the nest, they call to their mother. At this point she uncovers the tiny hatchlings and completes their release from the eggs, even carefully breaking the shells of any eggs that have not opened, so that the baby crocodiles can be released.

Now the mother gently picks up each baby in her mouth and carefully positions it in a special throat pouch. Any youngsters not correctly held are deftly tossed into the air and caught so that they can be positioned properly. When all the young are

Nile crocodiles, like all reptiles, regulate their body temperature according to the surrounding environment, often spending the whole day basking on riverbanks in the sun for heat, and gaping to release it through their mouths once they have become too hot.

secure, the mother transports them to a quiet backwater nursery area, where they are released and kept under her watchful eye. The young crocodiles soon learn to snap at insects and other small food items. They remain with their mother for several years, even clambering up to ride along on her back if danger threatens. They grow quickly when food is plentiful, gaining as much as 1ft (30 cm) in length in a year.

LEATHERBACK TURTLE
(*Dermochelys coriacea*)

The largest and heaviest of all the living turtles, and with extremely long fore flippers, leatherbacks are found in many warm parts of the ocean as they undertake huge journeys from their nesting beaches to their feeding areas in distant waters. Mainly tropical, they are also found in temperate and even subarctic waters on occasions. The leatherback is a pelagic creature in that it spends most of its life roaming the seas feeding on jellyfish, and only briefly comes ashore to lays its eggs.

At breeding time, males gather just offshore and attempt to mate with as many females as possible. Mating takes place in the water and the males take no further part in the breeding process once it is over. At night, each female swims to the shore and hauls herself laboriously up the beach, beyond the high-tide mark, to lay up to 150 or so eggs in a pit in the sand. She then covers these over with more sand, using her flippers, and slowly flaps her way back to the safety of the surf. The eggs take about 60 or 70 days to hatch. At nightfall, the tiny young turtles dig themselves up to the surface and begin their hazardous journey toward the safety of the sea. They waddle

and flap their way down the beach as fast as they can, but many fall prey to waiting seabirds, crabs and other predators. Even if they are able to reach the relative haven of the surf, many more are caught by fish and other animals. The hatchlings have scaly bodies at first, but soon this covering is replaced by the characteristic rubbery-looking shells of adult leatherback turtles.

There are two major leatherback feeding areas in the continental USA, one being a well-studied area near the mouth of the Columbia river, the other foraging area being located in the state of California.

CHAPTER THREE

BIRDS

OSTRICH (*Struthio camelus*)

The ostrich is the world's heaviest bird. It also lays the biggest eggs, at over 6in (15cm) long. It is a bird of the African savannah and semi-desert, where the wide open plains allow it the space to run at great speed to escape from its enemies. Ostriches live in flocks and feed on almost anything edible, but most of their food is vegetable matter. Figs and acacia seeds are favored items, but lizards, insects such as locusts, and even mice, appear on the menu.

At breeding time, a mature male holds sway over a breeding territory that includes several females. While the male is courting his females, he makes a communal scrape in his territory. After mating, he leads a female

to the scrape and she lays up to seven glossy white eggs; these are laid every other day for a period of two weeks. Other mated females also lay in the nest, adding their eggs to the clutch which may eventually number 50 eggs or so. However, only about half this number can be fully incubated, because the dominant female gathers her own eggs into the middle of the nest, pushing aside those of other females so that they are unlikely to hatch.

The female incubates the eggs by day, and the male sits on the nest at night. Incubation takes about three months. When first hatched, the chicks are covered in buff and darker speckled downy plumage to help conceal them against the sandy or stony ground. But within three months they have

grown feathers, although the full adult plumage is not acquired for about two years. By 18 months the chicks are fully grown, but until then they are brooded by their parents or even by other birds in the flock, which defend them against predators. During this time the chicks form a tight group, scuttling along behind several adults for protection. A mother and chicks may join other family units so that up to 100 or more chicks of varying ages may wander the plains with a number of adult birds.

Ostriches live in nomadic groups of five to 50 birds that often travel together with other grazing animals, such as zebras or antelopes. They are able to go without water for several days, surviving on the moisture of ingested plants.

EMPEROR PENGUIN
(*Aptenodytes forsteri*)

At about 4ft (1.2m) in height, the emperor penguin is the largest of the penguin species. The big, bulky body, dense plumage, and thick layer of body fat, are all adaptations for survival in the bleak, freezing Antarctic winter – the harshest conditions on Earth. The emperor penguin breeds on the sea ice that envelops the continent of Antarctica during the winter. The birds arrive in the breeding colonies in spring, following a bout of heavy feeding at sea to help tide them over the weather conditions to come. They leave the water and trek in long columns to the breeding colonies some 125 miles (200km) inland.

Pairs quickly form once the birds reach the colonies, and the females lay their single white egg in mid-May. Unlike most penguins, the emperor does not build a nest. Instead, the female lays her egg directly onto the ice. Almost at once, the male uses his bill to maneuver the egg onto the top of his own feet, where the egg comes into contact with his brood patch. This is a part of his belly that is bare of feathers and so allows the heat from his body to warm the egg. A loose fold of skin also envelops it, helping to insulate the egg against the intense cold.

Their egg-laying duties over, the females make the long trek back to the sea to feed. During this time, the males are left alone with their incubating egg until the females return with food some two months later. With no shelter, and with no prospect of food until their mates return, the males can only stand or waddle precariously about with their precious egg nestling between their feet, enduring the bitter, dark conditions. Frequently, the egg hatches before the female returns. The chick, which is almost naked at birth, is fed by the male with a regurgitated milk-like substance, although he is now in a fairly emaciated state. Once the female returns, however, he, too, can trek back to the sea to replenish himself with food.

As the young penguin chick grows, its body becomes covered in thick, gray, fluffy down feathers, although its head has the black-and-white plumage pattern of the adults. Soon the chick moves to join others, forming large groups or crèches of fat,

waddling chicks, that huddle together for warmth. They still rely on their parents for food, however, and call out using whistling sounds that are unique to each chick, making it possible for their parents to find them among the many other identical young penguins when they return from their long forays at sea. As summer approaches, they begin to assume their adult plumage, which they achieve after about 150 days. Soon it is time for the young penguins to make the journey to the sea themselves. Emperor penguins do not become sexually mature until they are three to six years old in the case of females – and up to nine years in males – so it will be some time before the young penguins make the journey back to the breeding grounds themselves.

It can take up to five months for a chick to molt into its juvenile plumage – often not completed by the time it leaves the colony; the adults cease feeding it during this time.

GREAT CRESTED GREBE
(*Podiceps cristatus*)

The great crested grebe is found over many parts of Europe and Asia as well as in parts of southern Africa and Australia, where it inhabits ponds, lakes, rivers and estuaries. It can often be spotted swimming on the surface, only to suddenly disappear and then resurface a little while later, grasping a slippery fish in its bill. As well as eating fish, grebes are seen on occasion feeding on their own feathers, and even offering them to their young. The purpose of this activity is to provide the intestines with protection against the sharp bones and scales of fish during the process

of digestion, the ball of feathers, together with the offending bones and scales, being later coughed up in the form of pellets.

Grebes begin to pair in winter. Their mating display involves the pair swimming toward each other, shaking their heads, each holding an embellishment of sorts in their beaks – usually a twig or piece of waterweed – and then rearing up in the water. This may go on for several weeks.

The nest is a floating mass of vegetation among reeds or a structure built up from the bottom of a lake. Usually, three to five dirty-white eggs are laid and incubated for 28 days. The fluffy chicks are gray-and-brown, with striped zebra-like black-and-white heads. Once hatched, they

Adult grebes are unmistakable in their summer plumage, with their striking head and neck decorations, but the young are remarkable, in that their heads are zebra-striped black-and-white. They lose these markings once they become adults.

leave the nest, spending the next few weeks hitching a ride on one of their parents' backs; this keeps them warm and safe, during which time they slowly learn how to catch fish for themselves, while still being fed by the parents. Fledging occurs after 70 to 80 days, during which time the young slowly acquire their adult plumage. Sometimes the breeding pair go on to produce another brood in the same season.

MUTE SWAN (*Cygnus olor*)

The stately mute swan is distinguished from other swans by its orange bill with its black knob at the base. These large birds frequent lakes, rivers and estuaries in many parts of the world, including Europe, Central Asia, China, North America, South Africa, New Zealand and Japan. With its long neck, the swan can upend in the water and feed on aquatic plants several feet down. It also feeds at the surface and sometimes takes frogs, insects and other aquatic animals. The opportunist nature of the mute swan is clearly evident at 'duck-feeding' time, when the birds muscle in to get the best of the offerings. It is not unusual for a swan to ungratefully accept pieces of bread offered by a human being, while at the same time hissing aggressively in defence of its young close by.

Mute swan pairs often bond for life. The territory – a large area of a lake or a mile (1.6km) or so of river – is defended

Young swans, known as cygnets, are not the bright white color of mature adults, and their bills are black rather than orange for the first year. The color of their down may range from gray to buff.

vigorously by the male, which chases away intruders with neck arched and wings held erect. The pair share in the building of the nest, which is a mound of vegetation usually positioned by the waterside, up to 3ft (1m) deep and 6ft (2m) across. Five to

seven green-tinged eggs are laid in the nest, and are incubated by the female for about 35 days, these being carefully covered with vegetation whenever she leaves the nest. Both parents share in the care of the newly-hatched young, or cygnets, which take to the water a couple of days after hatching. At first, the cygnets have short necks and gray-brown fluffy plumage. Sometimes they ride on their parents' back or hide beneath their wings for protection. As the young swans grow, they stay in close proximity with their parents. They keep their brown juvenile plumage until their second year, fledging at about 150 days.

MALLARD (*Anas platyrhynchos*)

The mallard is probably the world's most familiar and common wild duck, and is found over most of Europe as well as in North America and parts of Asia and Africa. They are often the main beneficiaries when people 'go feed the ducks,' swimming eagerly up close to the source of food to make sure they get the best of whatever is being offered, and even venturing to take food from the hand. Their natural diet consists of small water plants and aquatic animals, which the mallard sometimes gets by feeding at the surface and at other times by upending and stretching its neck to reach down for morsels of food.

Mallards spend most of their time on water, but can take off and land at very steep angles, which means they can inhabit quite small stretches of water with restricted access – one of the reasons why they are so common. They are found on lakes, small ponds, and streams and rivers. At breeding time, pairs nest alone or in small groups with others. The male is resplendent in his breeding plumage of shiny green head, white neck ring, and curly black tail-feathers. Most nests are built on the ground, near water, but some are constructed in the

crowns of low trees or in nest holes. The female lays six to 14 grey-green eggs at a rate of a few each day, until the clutch is complete. Once incubation begins, the male leaves to pursue other potential mates, and the job of hatching and rearing the young is undertaken by the female alone.

The eggs hatch after 27 or 28 days. Like the young of most ducks, the ducklings are born well-developed. This is so that they

can quickly leave the nest, where they are vulnerable to predators, and reach the relative safety of the water. The ducklings hatch out with fluffy brown-and-cream plumage and their eyes are open. Soon after they have all hatched, the young follow their mother from the nest down to the water, where they more or less fall in, bob to the surface, and immediately begin to swim. Thereafter, they follow their mother about everywhere, often swimming strung out in a line, and cheeping frequently. In the water, they learn to feed for themselves and spend time rearing up and flapping their tiny wings to help

strengthen the muscles they will need for flight. They grow fast, and fledge after about 50 or 60 days, but many young mallards never make it to adulthood. Predators take their toll, and others become traffic victims as they undertake perilous journeys back on land. Mallards become sexually mature at a year old.

Mallards frequently interbreed with their closest relatives, such as the American black duck, and also with species more distantly related, leading to various hybrids that may be fully fertile.

WOOD DUCK (*Aix sponsa*)

The attractive wood duck, or Carolina duck, is found in many parts of the eastern United States as well as in mid-west and western regions. They prefer wooded swamps, marshes, shallow ponds, and slow-moving river backwaters. Unlike many ducks, wood ducks have claws on their webbed feet, and this enables them to perch in trees; indeed, it is a requisite of these birds that there are trees close to the water, because they also nest in trees. Wood ducks search for seeds, nuts and aquatic plants which form the bulk of their diet.

The ducks pair and mate in early spring. The female chooses a site high up in a tree, the holes excavated by woodpeckers being a favorite choice. Between nine and 15 eggs are laid. When suitable nest sites are hard to find, it is not unusual for several other females to lay their eggs in a nest made by their neighbor, a practice known as 'egg dumping.' The preference is for a nest that overhangs the water, but nests up to 300ft (90m) or so from the water's edge are not uncommon. Incubation takes 30 days. Unusually for ducks, the male wood duck stays with the female during the incubation period, but leaves once the eggs have hatched.

After hatching, the young remain in the nest for about 24 hours. Then, one by one, the down-covered brown-and-gray ducklings clamber to the edge of the nest hole, using their tiny claws, and launch themselves out into the air. They cannot fly at this stage, but if the nest overhangs the water there should be a soft (but wet) landing in store. Otherwise, they simply drop to the ground, bounce upright, then

Wood ducks are year-round residents in east Texas and other southern parts of their range, but the northern populations migrate south for the winter, overwintering in the southern United States near to the Atlantic coast.

make their way to the water as quickly as possible, were they are joined by their mother. The young ducklings are able to feed themselves from the outset, and for a couple of weeks eat mainly insects and tiny fish. By about six weeks, however, they are feeding on waterweeds and other plants.

SNOWY OWL (*Bubo scandiacus*)

Ranging across the Arctic tundra in search of its prey, the snowy owl is found mainly in the cold northern zones of North America, Scandinavia and Asia. The bird has a thick covering of feathers to help insulate it against the bitter cold. Adult males are almost completely white, with a few dark markings, and females have dark-brown barred feathering, also longer talons. Both sexes have penetrating lemon-yellow eyes. Snowy owls prey on lemmings, voles, rabbits, gamebirds and even insects, which are seized in their sharp talons. Unlike other owls, hunting usually occurs during the daylight hours.

Because food is often scarce, snowy owls have large territories, and the male's mating calls carry for miles through the

Also known in North America as the Arctic owl or the great white owl, until recently the snowy owl was regarded as the sole member of a distinct genus, as Nyctea scandiaca, *but recent DNA testing shows it to be closely related to the genus Bubo.*

thin Arctic air. He performs swooping aerial displays over the chosen nest site, and also offers his prospective mate gifts of

lemmings to demonstrate his hunting skills, indicating how he will supply her with food once incubation starts. Tundra is treeless, and so the owls nest on the ground, making a scrape among vegetation. The female lays between three and nine eggs (occasionally more), and they are incubated for 31 to 33 days. Arctic foxes are one of the main enemies of nesting snowy owls, and in the event of one approaching, the female may try to lead it away from the nest by flapping away from it, pretending to be injured in the hope that the fox will follow.

Egg-laying is staggered by the hen, so that hatching will be at slightly different times, giving the older, stronger owlets an advantage if food is scarce. The young chicks, or owlets, hatch from the eggs using egg teeth to chip their way out. When first hatched, they are covered with thin, white downy feathers which, at about ten days, are replaced by sooty-gray feathers. The owlets leave the nest after four weeks but cannot fly at this stage; it takes about 50 days before they are fully fledged and begin to fly. By about 60 days the owlets are able to feed for themselves.

BARN OWL (*Tyto alba*)

The barn owl's piercing night shriek can be heard in farmland over much of the world. The birds prefer pastureland and grassland, and they need suitable old buildings and tree hollows in which to nest. Unfortunately, intensive farming has removed many suitable nest sites and reduced places where the owls can hunt their prey – which includes voles, mice, birds, reptiles, insects and frogs. Like most owls, the barn owl usually hunts by night or at dusk, being superbly adapted for the purpose and able to detect, thanks to its acute hearing, the slightest sound, following which the owl homes in on its prey, its large eyes gathering in all the available light. Special soft-fringed feathers, moreover, enable it to fly almost silently, so that the prey is usually unaware of the owl's approach. Then, as it swoops down, the owl grabs the victim in its great talons and carries it off.

Barn owls often nest in old farm buildings, where stored hay bales make ideal sites. The female lays about six eggs (sometimes a dozen or more), staggered at intervals of two or three days that will produce owlets of varying ages and sizes. The young hatch after about 33 days, and when food is brought by the parents the biggest get fed first, and so have the best chances of survival; but when times are hard, the youngest may even end up being eaten by their older siblings. The surviving owlets gradually change their fluffy white down into the beautiful white and golden-buff and gray adult plumage, a process which takes about 55 to 65 days.

With its ears placed asymmetrically for improved detection of sound, the Barn Owl has phenomenal hearing, and does not require sight to hunt; it targets then dives, seizing its prey with deadly accuracy.

HERRING GULL (*Larus argentatus*)

Widely seen in North America, Central America, Europe and Asia, where it is common around beaches and coastal cliffs and buildings, also frequently found inland in winter. An opportunist feeder, it is equally at home plucking fish and other marine life from the sea as it is soliciting seaside vacationers for food or scavenging among trash. The herring gull is heavily built, with a gray back and wings, and with white plumage on the rest of the body; the wings also have black tips and white spots. The strong bill is yellow with a red spot toward the tip.

Preferred nesting sites are cliff-tops, but seaside rooftops are also favored. The males

The American herring gull, Larus smithsonianus, *is a large gull, similar in appearance to* Larus argentatus, *except that immature birds tend to be darker and more uniformly brown.*

indulge in loud, raucous calls at mating time, that culminate in displays of neck-stretching. The nest is built from twigs and

other available materials, such as seaweed and grasses. The female lays two or three brown-blotched pale-green eggs, which are incubated by both sexes. The speckled brown-and-white chicks are fed on regurgitated meals by their parents, which are stimulated to provide these when the chicks peck at the red spot on the lower part of their bills. Juveniles fledge at about 35 to 40 days, at this time retaining a plumage with streaked brown feathers and darker-colored bills. It will be four years before they acquire the full coloration of the adult birds.

BLUE TIT (*Parus caeruleus*)

One of the most instantly recognizable of birds, the pretty blue tit frequents woods, parks and gardens, often appearing in flocks. The azure blue crown, and the dark-blue line passing through the eye and encircling the white cheeks to the chin, give the bird a very distinctive appearance. It is found all over Britain and Europe, as well as in North Africa and the Near East. Food consist of insects, caterpillars, nuts and seeds, which the birds often secure by means of remarkable acrobatic displays – hanging upside-down from bird-feeders being a favorite trick.

Preferred nest sites are holes in trees and other suitable places, and the bird is quite capable of enlarging a gap or crevice

in a house roof to make itself a comfortable nest; it also takes readily to nestboxes. The cup-shaped nest is built in early spring and is lined with moss, feathers, wool and animal hair. Egg-laying usually occurs in April and May, with up to 13 or so eggs sometimes being produced. The eggs are incubated by the female for about 12 to 16 days, and she is brought food by the male while performing this task. Once the eggs hatch, both parents share in the duties of feeding. On arrival at the nest with food, a parent is met with a daunting display of gaping mouths, all demanding food! The chicks fledge at about 19 days, with one after the other then making their first flight from the nest.

The blue tit is a valuable destroyer of garden pests, although it is not an entirely beneficial species, being also fond of young tree-buds, which it may pull to pieces in the hope of finding insects. No species, however, destroys more coccids and aphids, the worst foes of many plants, also leaf miner grubs.

CHAPTER FOUR

MAMMALS

VIRGINIA OPOSSUM
(*Didelphis virginiana*)

The Virginia opossum is the only marsupial found in North America and parts of Central America north of Mexico. A cat-sized mammal, it has short legs, a somewhat mouse-like head with a long, pointed muzzle, and white-flecked gray or brown fur. The tail is prehensile, which means it can be used to help grip branches as the animal clambers about.

These opossums are nocturnal and solitary for most of their lives, hunting for insects, fruits, small animals and eggs, and often raiding trash and refuse tips in search of food. They are fierce fighters, when cornered, but also have other tricks in reserve, giving a remarkable impression of being dead when all else fails – lying on their sides with their mouths open and remaining entirely motionless. They may keep up this pretence for hours, if necessary, exuding a foul anal fluid all the while. The term 'playing possum' derives from this strange but effective behavior.

The nest is built by packing leaves into tree hollows. The female produces one or two litters a year, each initially comprising

up to 18 young, born after about a 12-day gestation period. Virginia opossums are marsupials, which means that the young are born in a very undeveloped state, completing their growth in a special pouch, or marsupium. In the pouch, they fasten onto teats and are fed milk, although only about seven or so young survive. These are weaned at about three months, when they abandon the pouch, and for the next four to six weeks travel about clinging onto their mother's back for safety.

The Virginia opossum is the original 'opossum,' the word coming from the Algonquian meaning 'white animal.' Australia's possums, named thus from their similarity to the Virginia opossum, are also marsupials, but of the order Diprotodontia.

KOALA (*Phascolarctos cinereus*)

Looking rather like a comical, ragged-eared bear, the endearing koala is a favorite with people everywhere. It is another marsupial mammal, giving birth to tiny young that continue their development within a pouch on the mother's body. This tree-dwelling animal seldom leaves the safety of its eastern Australian arboreal

home, where its diet consists almost entirely of eucalyptus leaves and shoots.

The koala lives singly or in small groups, with a male usually gathering together a harem of several females. Breeding occurs in the summer, with the female producing a tiny, single young after a month's gestation. As soon as it is born, the young koala makes its way to the pouch, where it fastens onto a teat, remaining there for five or six months. It then leaves the pouch, but continues to be carried about on its mother's back for a further four to five months. After weaning, the young koala is fed a diet of semi-digested leaves.

Although taxonomically incorrect, the name koala bear is still used outside of Australia, where it was adopted because of the animal's passing likeness to a Teddy bear.

COMMON WOMBAT
(*Vombatus ursinus*)

The common wombat is a sturdy, somewhat badger-like marsupial mammal found in the forests and scrublands of eastern Australia and Tasmania. It has gray-brown fur, a broad head with short ears, and a very short tail. Since this is a burrowing animal, the feet are strong and extremely well-clawed, and it builds extensive tunnel systems that may stretch for distances of 40ft (12m) or more underground. This is an herbivorous animal, feeding mainly on grasses, for which its intestines are specially adapted.

The female gives birth to the young in the autumn: usually, one baby is born, which makes its way to the mother's pouch. Here it secures its mouth to one of two teats and remains in the pouch, being nourished on the mother's milk for about

*The Bass Strait subspecies (*Vombatus ursinus ursinus*) is found only on Flinders Island to the north of Tasmania. It is listed as vulnerable by the Environment Protection and Biodiversity Conservation Act 1999, and is on the World Conservation Union's Red List.*

three months. Once the young wombat leaves the pouch, it forages for food with its mother for a further few months before setting off to live independently.

WHIPTAIL WALLABY
(*Macropus parryi*)

Also known as the Blue or Grey Flier and Pretty-Face wallaby, it is easy to see why the latter should be so. The whiptail is distinguishable from other wallabies in that it has a very long, thin tail that it swishes with a whip-like action. Whiptail wallabies have light-brown to gray coats, with defined markings of black and white on their faces, white-tipped ears, and white stripes that run over the hips.

The female becomes sexually mature at about 18 to 24 months, but young males rarely get the chance to mate until they are two to three, due to the dominant male of the group keeping the younger ones at bay. Whiptail wallabies give birth in January, after a five-week pregnancy. After birth, the tiny joey crawls into its mother's pouch and suckles one of her four teats, remaining there until it reaches eight or nine months, but continuing to nurse until it is about 15 months old. The joey reaches maturity at about two years of age, when it will begin to move away from its mother's side.

These are social animals that live in groups of up to 50, being most abundant in northern New South Wales and southern Queensland, but also to be found farther north as far as Cooktown. Whiptails live mainly on grasses, ferns and small native plants, feeding during hot weather in the early mornings and late afternoons. They rest in the shade during the hottest part of the day, but in cooler temperatures carry on feeding throughout the day. Their preferred habitat is undulating or hilly country with open forests and areas of grass.

The whiptail wallaby rarely drinks water except in extreme drought. It gets all it needs from the vegetation it consumes.

EASTERN GRAY KANGAROO
(*Macropus giganteus*)

Also known as great grays and forester kangaroos, eastern grays looks much like their relatives, the red kangaroo, despite being slightly smaller, and grow to a height of 5–6ft (1.5–1.8m). They have small heads with large ears, and the fur is somewhat coarser and curlier than that of the western gray. The color varies from gray to brown with white underparts, legs, and underside of tail. The tail is 4ft (1.2m) long and very strong, and it is used for balance while running and as a prop when the animal is standing upright. The hind legs are muscular, and the hind feet are long and very broad, contrasting with the fore legs which are short; these end in small, hand-like feet with five digits that are able to grasp objects. The females hold their young in their pouches until they are mature, communicating with them by means of squeaks and clucks.

Eastern grays reach sexual maturity at around 18 months to two years of age. The breeding season is from spring to early summer, and the joey is born after a short gestation period of 30–38 days, emerging from the birth canal when it is only an inch (2.5cm) long. It then crawls into the mother's pouch and fixes itself onto a teat, remaining there for almost a year. It will continue to nurse after it has left the pouch, and will keep on doing so until it is about 18 months old.

In Australian parlance, adult male kangaroos are known as 'boomers' and the females as 'does,' while juveniles are called 'fliers' and the babies 'joeys.' Social groups are formed, known as 'mobs,' that are dominated by matriarchal females, together with other females and their young.

TWO-TOED SLOTH
(*Choloepus didactylus*)

Few animals are as perfectly at home in the trees as the two-toed sloth. It spends almost its entire life suspended upside-down from the branches, hanging on with its enormous hooked claws. It is so adapted to this upside-down world that even its hair grows the wrong way up. The hair is tinged green from the algae that festoon it, and this helps to give the sloth a degree of camouflage among the leaves of the South American forests. It eats, sleeps, defecates and even gives birth hanging upside-down. The sloth moves slowly and purposefully about in its arboreal habitat, eating leaves, fruits and twigs. It moves even more slowly on the ground, dragging itself along, although it it able to swim quite well. It is mostly nocturnal.

Sloths breed throughout the year, the females giving birth to a single young after a gestation period of about 260 days. The young sloths, of course, are also adapted to life above the ground, and cling securely to their mother for about a month. They remain clinging to her for a further six months or more, after they have been weaned, all the while helping themselves to leaves from the surrounding branches.

OPPOSITE: A baby sloth clings for dear life onto its mother.

ABOVE: This juvenile is already confident fending for itself among the branches.

95

EUROPEAN HEDGEHOG
(*Erinaceus europaeus*)

Unfortunately, most hedgehog sightings are as roadside casualties, yet this prickly mammal is a frequent nocturnal visitor to suburban gardens, where it can be heard snuffling around in the undergrowth for worms and other invertebrates. The upper part of the hedgehog's head and body is covered in spines, the animal simply rolling itself into a tight, spiky ball when danger threatens, making it an unwelcome meal prospect for a potential predator. The hedgehog's range includes Britain and many other parts of Europe, including Scandinavia, where its more natural home comprises hedgerows and woodland edges.

The European hedgehog produces one, sometimes two, litters per year, depending on weather conditions. Each litter consists of about five young, born into a breeding nest made of leaves, grasses and twigs, after a 35-day gestation period. The tiny deaf and blind baby hedgehogs are born with their prickles, but these are confined beneath the skin during birth to avoid damaging the mother's birth canal. The prickles emerge, white in color, a few hours later. The young are weaned at about five weeks, and they can roll themselves into protective balls by the time they are two or three weeks old. After weaning, the young seek out as much food as they can in readiness for the coming winter hibernation.

Hedgehogs are named for their pig-like habit of rooting through undergrowth for food. They are quite noisy and can be heard snuffling and grunting during their activities.

GREATER FRUIT BAT OR INDIAN FLYING FOX (*Pteropus giganteus*)

With a wingspan of about 5ft (1.5m), this is the largest species of bat. Fruit bats are often known as flying foxes because many have brown or reddish fur and fox-like faces. The greater fruit bat is found in the forests of southern and South-East Asia, where it lives in large groups. Flocks consisting of thousands of these animals roost by day in large trees, but take to the air in a dense cloud of beating wings to look for food as night falls. The bat has peg-like teeth with which it crushes fruit, such as mangoes, to obtain the available nutriment, spitting out the seeds at the same time.

This species is polygynandrous, with no pair bonds occurring between males and females. Females are defended from intruders by males that live in their roosting tree. Mating takes place from July to October, with the female usually vocalizing and physically resisting the advances of the male during the encounter. The young are born from February to May, after a gestation period of about 140 days. One or two young are born, which are carried around by the mother for the first three weeks or so of their life. They begin to hang onto branches by themselves after this time, although they are still transported to feeding sites by their mother. The young are weaned at five months. Males play no part in caring for their infants.

RIGHT: Baby fruit bats are transported around by their mother until they are strong enough to hang from branches themselves.

*OPPOSITE: There are many types of fruit bat: pictured here is a family of black flying foxes (*Pteropus alecto*) from Australia.*

RINGTAILED LEMUR (*Lemur catta*)

This primate gets its name from its distinctive, bushy, black-and-white tail, which accounts for over half the animal's total length. The head has a pointed muzzle, large bright eyes, and triangular ears. The ringtailed lemur is found only on the island of Madagascar, as are all other lemurs, this particular one being a native of southern Madagascar, where it lives in dry, rocky terrain with scattered trees.

Groups of these lemurs, known as troops, consist of about 20 individuals, although this may rise to 40 or so on occasions. The animals are active by day and occupy a territory, marking it frequently with scent from special glands found on many parts of the body. Females and young form the basis of the troop, with males moving from one troop to another. This is a matriarchal society, highly unusual in primates, and females are dominant over males. The ringtailed lemur eats mainly fruit, bark and leaves.

The female gives birth to one young, sometimes two, after a gestation period of about 120 days. The young are born with a good covering of fur and with their eyes open. Initially, they cling to their mother's underside as she moves about the territory, but after two weeks switch to riding on her back. By six months the young lemurs are able to find food for themselves.

The name lemur was selected by early biologists because the calls of some elusive lemur species were claimed to evoke the cries of the spirits of the dead or the lemures *of Roman mythology. The species' name,* catta, *arose from the similarity between the ringtailed lemur's purring vocalization and that of the domestic cat.*

GREATER GALAGO (BUSHBABY)
(*Otolemur crassicaudatus*)

Bushbabies, or galagos, are part of a group of primates found in Africa and southern Asia. Especially in the breeding season, the greater bushbaby makes a call that resembles a child crying, and this gave rise to the animal's common name. Found in countries such as Somalia, Kenya and South Africa, where it inhabits forests, savannah and plantations, the bushbaby is an adept climber and spends much of its life in the trees. Its hands and feet are adapted to help it grasp firmly onto branches, and its large eyes and big, sensitive ears help it to locate its food.

The bushbaby is active at night, feeding on a variety of items such as reptiles, birds and their eggs, and insects. A rapid lunge to grab the prey is followed by a quick bite to dispatch it. Bushbabies usually live in groups consisting of a mother and her young. They move about on their own when feeding, but often join other groups to sleep together during the day. They frequently scent-mark their routes and territories.

Females give birth to one to three young between May and October, with each newborn weighing less than half an ounce (14g). For the first few days after birth, the mother keeps the infants with her all the time, picking them up with her hands or mouth, and letting them cling to her. Later, she sometimes leaves them in the nest, usually built into the fork of a tree, while she goes off hunting. The young are weaned after six weeks and can feed themselves at two months. They grow quickly, making it quite difficult by now for the mother to carry them about.

Bushbabies are relatively common and are under no immediate danger of extinction.

GOLDEN SNUB-NOSED MONKEY *(Rhinopithecus roxellana)*

This is an Old World monkey, endemic to a small area in temperate mountainous forests of central China, primarily around the Sichuan basin, where its Chinese name is the Sichuan golden-haired monkey. Snow occurs frequently within the monkey's range and it can withstand colder average temperatures than any other non-human primate. Its diet varies markedly with the seasons, but it is primarily a herbivore with lichens being its main source of food. It is diurnal and largely arboreal, spending some 97 per cent of its time in the forest canopy. Population estimates range from 8,000 to 15,000 and it is endangered by reason of loss of its habitat.

Distribution of the golden snub-nosed monkey is limited to the mountains of four Chinese provinces: Sichuan, Gansu, Shaanxi, and Hubei. Although these protected areas are far greater than is required for the survival of such a species, they are in reality much smaller; this is because the monkeys heavily depend on dense forests, which due to illegal logging and environmental destruction have been reduced to only one fifth of their total area.

Relatively little is known of these elusive creatures, although recent studies have revealed many aspects of their behavior and ecology. They are highly social animals, forming units of 20–30 in winter, which often join into larger troops of up to 200 in summer, while several of these groups may temporarily combine to form enormous bands of up to 600. These larger groups are sub-divided into smaller

Research on the golden snub-nosed monkey has mostly taken place at the Shennongjia and Baihe Nature Reserves in the Hubei and Sichuan provinces respectively.

family units, comprising a dominant male and around four females with their young. Females mature sexually at four to five, and males when they are seven years old. Mating can occur throughout the year, but August, September and October are the peak periods, and young are often born in March or April but sometimes in February and May, following a gestation period of six months.

VERVET MONKEY
(*Chlorocebus pygerythrus*)

This small, black-faced monkey ranges throughout much of southern and eastern Africa, and from Ethiopia and Somalia south to South Africa.

There are several sub-species of vervet monkey, but generally the body is a greenish-olive or silvery-gray in color, the face, ears, hands, feet and tail-tip being black, while a conspicuous white band on the forehead blends in with the short whiskers. The males are slightly larger than

the females and easily recognized by their turquoise-blue and red genitalia.

The vervet is classified as a medium-sized to large monkey, with males weighing up to 17lbs (8kg). Tails are usually held up,

with the tip curving downward. Arms and legs are approximately the same length.

Vervet society is built on complex but stable social groups (troops) of 10–50 individuals, mainly adult females and their immature offspring. There is a strict hierarchy, and a mother's social standing predetermines that of her offspring; even adults in a family must submit to juveniles of families with higher social status. Males

From fresco artworks found in Akrotiri on the Mediterranean island of Santorini, there is evidence that the vervet was known there in around 2000 BC, this being evidence of early contact between Egypt and the island.

change troops at least once in their lifetime, beginning at puberty; this is a dangerous process not only because of the predators they may encounter in transit, but also because existing troops dislike newcomers.

Grooming is important in a monkey's life, and vervets (as do most other primates) spend several hours a day removing parasites, dirt or other material from one another's fur, with dominant individuals getting the most grooming. The hierarchical system also controls feeding, mating, fighting, friendships, and even survival.

Close social bonds with female relatives begin to develop in infancy, relationships thought to endure throughout life. Infants are of great interest to other monkeys in the troop, and young females vie to be allowed to groom or hold a new infant.

After a birth, the mother licks the infant clean, bites off the umbilical cord, then consumes the afterbirth. The newborn has black hair and a pink face, and it will be three or four months before it acquires full adult coloration.

The infant spends the first week of life clinging to its mother's belly. After about the third week it begins to move about by itself and attempts to play with other young monkeys. Vervet mothers are possessive toward their babies, and most are loath to let other young or even adult females hold or carry them, while others will gladly leave their infants with any interested female, although it is believed that a female's close family will usually have the most unrestricted access. As the infants grow, they play not only with their peers but also with other young animals in their environment.

Vervet monkeys seems to possess the rudiments of language, with alarm calls varying in accord with different types of threats made to the community.

JAPANESE MACAQUE
(*Macaca fuscata*)

In the high-altitude forests of Japan lives the country's only primate, the Japanese macaque. Apart from human beings, no other primate can survive in such a near-freezing climate, and to help it survive the harsh conditions it is often found wallowing in warm thermal pools, which it stays in for hours on end, immersed up to its neck. A monkey of medium build, with long whiskers, beard, and dense fur, it is active both in the trees and on the ground, feeding on bark, berries, nuts, buds and leaves, as well as on insects.

Groups of about 40 individuals live together, with an older male as the leader.

The Japanese macaque, also known as the snow monkey, is the most northern-living non-human primate. It is a terrestrial Old World species native to Japan, although an introduced free-ranging population has been living near Laredo, Texas, since 1972.

Within the macaque community there is a well-developed relationship and bond

between mothers and their daughters, which remain strong even when the younger animals have offspring of their own. Males stay with the troop until adolescence, after which they go off to find another to join.

Males and females have multiple partners during the breeding season, with sexual maturity having been reached at about three years of age. Gestation lasts for about five to six months, and each female produces one baby at a time, with the peak periods of birth occurring in May to September and April to July. As with other primates, infants are slow to grow and develop, and their dependence on parents can be long and often stressful. Weaning takes a full year, and during this time the mother needs to protect the young as well as feed it. Males, however, help in the task, carrying the young around, cuddling, grooming and protecting them. Sometimes other, non-parental adults share in the task of rearing the young. All this time the young learn how to interact with the group, using a combination of facial expressions, body postures, sounds, and physical contact occurring in grooming and play.

SUMATRAN ORANGUTAN
(*Pongo abelii*)

One of the most charismatic of the great apes, the orangutan is a large, long-armed primate with long, reddish hair. This species inhabits the island of Sumatra in Indonesia, and is truly arboreal, in that it seldom leaves the safety of the trees, where it moves about with grace and ease using a combination of clambering and swinging maneuvers. It occurs in lowland forests and wooded swamplands, building a nest of bent branches and leaves in which to rest and sleep for the night. The Sumatran orangutan lives

The Sumatran orangutan is the rarer of the two species of orangutan, the other being the smaller Pongo pygmaeus, *a native of the island of Borneo.*

in small groups, roaming about looking for seasonal fruits such as figs, also flowers, bark and the occasional bird's egg.

Most mating occurs when fruits are in full season, usually in the rainy period between December and May, and any female not already caring for an offspring is available. Females usually give birth to a single young, occasionally twins, following a gestation period of around 250 days. Once a female has given birth, she spends the next eight or nine years looking after her young.

This is a great and unique commitment for an animal, especially as it is the female that must undertake the rearing, with the male taking no part in the process. The mother carries the baby around with her while it is small, and provides it with all its food, giving her milk until the baby is weaned, following which she provides food for it from the forest. She teaches the young orangutan how to feed on over 400 kinds of food, the types of social behavior used by orangutans, and how to communicate with others of its kind. Orangutans use their expressive faces to give a range of signals, so there is much to learn. Grooming includes the mother trimming the youngster's toenails by biting off the excess length.

CHIMPANZEE (*Pan troglodytes*)

Intelligent and sociable, the chimpanzee is *Homo sapiens'* nearest living relative. It has been much studied over many years, both in the wild and in captivity, and continues to be an important subject in the quest for our understanding of how animals learn skills, behave, and interact with others of their kind. Unfortunately, our own relationship with the chimpanzee, as with so many other animals, has often been cruel and exploitative, not the least of which has been the destruction of many important parts of the chimpanzee's habitat in the wild.

Chimpanzees are found in the rainforests and wooded savannahs of West and Central Africa, from Gambia to Uganda, but with some interrupted distribution in between. Robust and strongly built, the chimpanzee has long limbs with particularly powerful forearms. The animal is adept at clambering and swinging through the trees, but actually spends most of its time on the ground,

where it usually walks on all fours; when its hands are full, however, it will resort to walking on its back legs. Chimpanzees live in groups, or troops, the composition of which varies. It may consist of males only, females and young, or adults of both sexes and young. These animals have an advanced social structure which includes complex hierarchies, co-operation in finding and capturing food, many different forms of communication, including facial expressions, vocalizations and body postures, and breeding. Active by day, their food ranges from fruit, nuts, seeds, shoots and bark, to eggs, insects and other animals. Like orangutans, chimpanzees have learned to use tools to obtain some of their food: for example, twigs inserted into nests are used to extract the termites within. A troop may also co-operate to catch animals such as bush pigs and other monkeys.

Chimpanzees may breed throughout the year, and multiple partners are commonplace. Gestation lasts for an average of 230 days, and one, sometimes

two, young are born. Like other primates, the young must receive constant care for some time, the newborn being carried around for three to six months, after which time it usually rides on its mother's back; as it grows, however, it may walk around by itself for periods at a time. Weaning takes between 30 to 54 months. Females provide much of the parental care, grooming, feeding and nursing. They also provide the youngster with the social interactive skills it will require to enable it to communicate with others of its kind and develop the full range of chimpanzee behavior. The young are entirely dependent on their mother until weaned, but stay with her until adulthood, which occurs at the age of about ten years. Bonds between siblings produced by the same mother are also well-developed.

When confronted by a predator, chimpanzees will react with loud screams and use any object they can fnd to fight off the threat.

GORILLA (*Gorilla gorilla*)

The largest of all the great apes, this mighty and impressive primate is divided into several subspecies, all of which are found in the forests of equatorial Africa from sea level to 13,000ft (4000m). The gorilla has black fur, although in older males the hair on the back and rump turns gray, resulting in such animals being known as 'silverbacks.' Gorillas have no tail. Despite its formidable appearance and huge jaws, this animal is shy and peace-

Mountain gorillas inhabit the Albertine Rift montane cloud forests of the Virunga Mountains, while lowland gorillas live in the dense forests and lowland swamps and marshes that lie at sea level.

loving unless threatened, and is essentially
herbivorous, eating leaves, berries and
bark. The animals are active during the
day, and much of their food is taken on the
ground, although they sometimes climb
trees to gain access to other food items.

They live in groups of between five and
15 individuals, each consisting of a
dominant male with females and their
young. Day and night nests are constructed
from branches and leaves. Because of the
abundance of food in their chosen areas,
gorillas do not spend much time and
energy moving from place to place.

It is usual for the dominant male to
mate with all the females in the gorilla

troop. There is no fixed breeding season, and after mating a single baby is born after a nine-month gestation period. It weighs about 4.5lbs (2kg) at birth. The young gorilla is nursed for three to four years and is dependent on its mother during that time; but the mother sometimes abandons one in favor of the other if she has more than one young. The baby is able to cling to its mother and crawl about by the time it is three months old. Females within the troop also provide transport, protection and food for the baby; they also socialize it and prepare it to lead an eventual independent life.

GRAY WOLF (*Canis lupus*)

The gray (grey) wolf ranges widely across Eurasia (including India), North America and Mexico, although its populations and distribution are now much restricted in certain places, due to habitat destruction and the inevitable interaction with human beings; it is now found only in a handful of American states, Wisconsin and Michigan being two such examples. Powerful and muscular, and the stuff of legends that go back centuries, the wolf is feared yet admired in equal measure. It is intelligent and sociable, and lives in groups called packs that may include members of more than one family. The pack hunts together, with each member participating in the running down of prey, which consists of deer, caribou and smaller animals such as rats, mice and fish.

In the gray wolf, coloration varies from gray to gray-brown and through all the canine spectrum of white, red, brown, and black. Colors tend to be mixed in many populations, though it is not uncommon for individuals or entire populations to be one color, usually all black or all white.

BABY ANIMALS

The pack hierarchy is strictly maintained by a complex system of social signals and gestures, and a dominant individual, usually a female, rules the pack. Mating takes place from January until April, and the pups are born after a gestation period of nine weeks. Litters consist of between two and ten pups. At birth, the cubs are blind, deaf and entirely dependent on their mother, remaining in a den – often a tunnel in a hillside – for two months after birth. In time the cubs become more independent and start to explore their immediate surroundings. To begin with, they feed on the mother's milk,

but later also begin to take regurgitated food. The cubs are so well-integrated into the pack, after a couple of months, that some pack members look after them while the rest go on hunting forays. When bigger, they will join the hunting pack, although initially only as observers. While feeding on the spoils, they begin to contest for food with each other, which helps them learn the pack rules concerning hierarchy, dominance and submission. They also indulge in play fighting, which develops their true fighting skills and also helps them to understand pack 'rules.' At about three years, many of the young wolves leave the pack to form territories of their own.

ARCTIC FOX (*Alopex lagopus*)

The Arctic fox is truly at home in the harsh conditions of northern Eurasia and North America. In winter, its gray-brown coat turns white, which helps it to remain concealed among the snow and ice as it hunts its prey of small mammals (such as lemmings) and ground-dwelling birds, although it may eat berries as well. Its well-furred feet and small, heat-retaining ears are other cold-climate adaptations, for the Arctic fox does not hibernate.

The gestation period for these animals is between 50 and 56 days. Litters tend to be six or seven cubs, but up to 11 or even more have been known. The cubs are a

The Arctic fox has evolved to survive some of the harshest conditions on the planet, having adaptations that include deep, thick fur, a system of countercurrent heat exchange in the circulation of the paws to retain core temperature, and a good supply of body fat.

brownish color at birth. Both parents take their turn caring for and rearing the young, which are kept in the safety of a den, this usually being an underground complex of tunnels. Siblings from a previous year's litter will often stay with the parents and help look after the newly born. Weaning takes about two to four weeks, after which time the young emerge from the den.

RED FOX (*Vulpes vulpes*)

The red fox has the widest distribution throughout the world of any member of the dog family, the Canidae, being found throughout much of the northern hemisphere from the Arctic to Central America, central Asia and northern Africa, and it has also been introduced elsewhere. Persecuted by farmers everywhere, the red fox has nevertheless flourished, being an intelligent and opportunist feeder. It is equally adept at catching mice and large insects in meadows as it is raiding suburban areas for food scraps discarded by humans.

The mating period varies with location, but ranges from December through to the following April. Courtship is a noisy business, and there is much barking and screeching. Gestation lasts about 50 days, with litter sizes varying from one to 13 cubs, although the average is about five.

The red fox is mostly nocturnal, although it will sometimes venture out during the day. It stalks its prey much like a cat, stealthily coming within range before pouncing on the unfortunate victim.

The cubs are born blind, but open their eyes nine to 14 days after birth, born into the safety of an underground earth, or den. The female guards them while the male goes out hunting for food. The cubs leave the den four or five weeks after birth and are weaned by eight to ten weeks. They will often be seen near the den's entrance, in play practising the pouncing and fighting techniques they will adopt for real when fully grown. Then the cubs accompany their mother on forays, as they learn the techniques of hunting. The cubs stay with their mother until the autumn following their birth, after which time they disperse to form their own territories.

COYOTE (*Canis latrans*)

The ubiquitous coyote is a member of the dog family, found in all parts of North and Central America, and in all but the northernmost parts of Canada. They make their dens in rocky crevices, caves, or the deserted lairs of other animals which they may enlarge. Desert coyotes are light gray or tan with a black tip to the tail, while mountain coyotes have darker, thicker and longer fur, with underparts that are nearly white, with some specimens having a white tip to the tail. In winter, the coats of mountain coyotes become long and silky, and trappers hunt them for their fur.

Female coyotes remain in heat for two to five days between late January and late March, during which time mating occurs. Once the female chooses a partner, the mated pair may remain temporarily monogamous for a number of years. The gestation period lasts from 60 to 65 days, and litter size can range from one to 19

Coyotes usually flourish in areas where wolves have been exterminated. As New England became increasingly settled, for example, and the resident wolves were eliminated, the coyote population increased, filling the empty biological niche. Coyotes also appear better equipped to live among people than wolves.

pups, although the average is 6. These large litters act as compensation against the high juvenile mortality rate, with approximately

50–70 per cent of pups failing to survive into adulthood. The pups are born blind, but their eyes open after about 14 days and they emerge from the den a few days later. They suckle for five to seven weeks, and begin to take semi-solid food after three weeks. While the father helps support the babies with his regurgitated food, the mother prevents him from coming all the way into the den.

The pups live and play in the den until they are six to ten weeks old, when the mother begins to take them out hunting in a group. Then the family gradually begins to disband, and the pups are usually hunting alone by the fall. Within a year they are ready to go their own way, when they will stake out their own territory and mark it with their scent. Although coyotes have been seen traveling in large groups,

they primarily hunt in pairs, with typical packs consisting of six closely-related adults, yearlings and young. Coyote packs are generally smaller than those of wolves, and associations between individuals are less stable, possibly due to earlier expressions of aggression and the fact that coyotes reach their full growth in their first year, unlike wolves, which reach maturity in their second.

POLAR BEAR (*Ursus maritimus*)

The heaviest of the bear species (adult males can weigh 1,500lbs/680kg), the polar bear is found all around the Arctic region surrounding the North Pole, being unmistakable with its white fur, tiny ears, and black-tipped nose. Carnivorous and dangerous, the bear feeds mainly on seals, for which it often lies in wait as they come up to breathe through holes in the ice, but also on walruses, seabirds and other smaller animals. It may wander for miles across ice floes, often swimming long distances in the sea as well. Nowadays, reduction in the pack ice, due to climate changes and competition for their food sources, has forced them increasingly to encroach on human habitation, and they are frequently seen scavenging for food.

The polar bear leads a solitary existence for most of the year. Breeding usually takes place from early to late spring, with the fertilized egg remaining in

Although it is now a highly vulnerable species, the polar bear has for thousands of years been a key figure in the material, spiritual, and cultural life of indigenous Arctic peoples.

a suspended state until September or October. During these months, the pregnant female consumes prodigious amounts of food, gaining at least 440lbs (200kg) and often more than doubling her body weight. The young – typically two cubs – are born in a covered snow den about two or three months later. At this stage their eyes are closed and they have only a very fine covering of body fur. Within the safe haven of the den, they are fed on their mother's milk until March or April, by which stage they are big enough to venture out onto the ice. The cubs may stay with their mother for about two-and-a-half years, learning to hunt before they set off to establish their own territories. They reach sexual maturity at about five or six years of age.

BROWN BEAR (*Ursus arctos*)

The brown, or grizzly, bear has its major strongholds in Russia, Canada and Alaska, although it once ranged over a much larger area, venturing as far as North Africa and Mexico and into areas such as mainland Europe and Britain. Brown bears are found in forests, tundra and semi-desert. Another very large and dangerous member of the ursine species, the brown bear has a wide-ranging diet that includes berries, fruits, insects, fish, rodents and livestock. At over 9ft (2.7m) in length, this is a massive creature, towering over other animals when standing up on its back legs.

Females typically breed every two to four years, making them not always available for mating, so males fight vigorously with each other for the right to mate, which occurs from May to July. By a delayed process, the female's fertilized egg divides and floats free within the uterus for six months, and during winter dormancy will become attached to the uterine wall, the cubs being born after an eight-week period while the mother sleeps. Two to three offspring are usually produced, born with their eyes closed and sparsely furred. The cubs feed on their mother's milk for a period of up to 30 months, although they are taking a wide range of other foods by the time they are five months old. The cubs remain with their mother until their second spring, but often until their third or fourth. The mother is attentive but aggressive in defence of her young, but the male takes no part at all in looking after the cubs.

Today, there are three genetically distinct brown bear clades in North America: the Alaskan-Yukon, the Alberta-Saskatchewan, and that of the Colorado-Washington-Idaho-Montana-Wyoming area.

AMERICAN BLACK BEAR
(*Ursus americanus*)

This is the most common bear species relative to North America. It is found throughout much of Canada and the United States (except the central plains region) and also in Mexico. It frequents a range of habitats from dense forest to brushland. An omnivore, its diet includes berries, nuts, shoots, and fish, and being quite large, it can also take deer and other similar animals. Usually black, but also cinnamon, brown or even blue-gray or blond, the bear has a pale muzzle and less heavily furred ears than the brown, or grizzly, bear. It is also smaller at 6ft (1.8m) in length.

Mating usually occurs from May to July, with egg implantation occurring in the autumn. Births usually take place in the following January or February, with litter sizes being about three on average, although they can be as much as six. The young are born blind, and they remain in the den with their mother for the remainder of the winter, feeding on her milk. The cubs, with their mother, emerge in spring,

There were once probably as many as two million black bears in North America, which declined to a low of 200,000 as a result of habitat destruction and unrestricted hunting. By current estimates, more than 800,000 are now living on the continent today.

and weaning continues until they are about six to eight months old. The young stay with their mother until they are about 18 months, in the meantime learning the hunting skills necessary for life on their own. It is at this stage that the mother forces them from the territory.

RED PANDA (*Ailurus fulgens*)

This attractive animal inhabits the upland temperate deciduous and coniferous forests of the Himalayas in northern Burma, Nepal and south-west China. Like the giant panda, the red panda cannot digest cellulose, so it must consume vast amounts of bamboo in order to survive, although it also eat berries, fruits, roots, acorns, lichens and grasses, and is known to take young birds, fish, eggs, small rodents, and insects on occasions. The animal's tail is marked with alternating red-

Unlike the giant panda, the red panda is not a bear, and recent DNA research now places it into its own independent family Ailuridae, loosely encompassing skunks, raccoons and weasels.

and-buff rings, and the head has a white muzzle, ear fringes, eyebrows and cheek patches. The rest of the body is reddish-brown on the back and sides, with black on the belly and legs. Mainly active at night, the arboreal red panda moves easily through the trees, using its tail for balance.

Mating takes place in winter, with the young arriving in June after a gestation period of about 134 days. In preparation for the birth, the mother starts to build a nest using grasses, sticks and leaves, siting it in a hollow tree or a crevice in a rock. Once the young are born (the litter being usually one to four cubs), the mother cleans them up and remains with them almost constantly for the first few days of their life. After a week or so, she begins to leave them for longer periods, only returning to the nest to clean it and to feed and groom her babies. After about 90 days the young leave the nest for the first time under the cover of darkness, guarded by their ever-watchful mother. They stay with her for about 18 months, the father playing little part in the rearing of his young.

RACCOON (*Procyon lotor*)

Raccoons are most commonly found across southern Canada, in most of the United States, and through to the northern parts of South America. Their preferred habitat is moist woodland, but these are extremely adaptable animals which have learned to exploit human habitation. They are often seen scavenging around urban areas and delving into garbage bins, making their 'masked bandit'

appearance seem particularly appropriate. Stocky and agile, with gray fur and a black-ringed bushy tail, the raccoon is mainly active at night, clambering around in vegetation and even swimming when necessary. Its natural food consists of frogs, fish, rodents, birds and their eggs, nuts, seeds and corn.

A litter usually comprises between one and seven young, born after a gestation period of around 64 days. The young, born blind and helpless in an arboreal den, are

As a result of escapes and deliberate introductions in the mid-20th century, raccoons are now seen across the European mainland, the Caucasus, and Japan.

weaned after about 70 days, and by about 20 weeks are able to leave the nest to join their mother on nocturnal foraging expeditions. They stay with her through the first winter, becoming independent by the following spring, although they may build their dens close to that of their mother.

GIANT PANDA

(*Ailuropoda melanoleuca*)

The rare, endangered and iconic giant panda is found only in a few central provinces of China, where it inhabits mixed deciduous and coniferous mountain forests where bamboo also grows. This is vital, since bamboo leaves and stalks form over 90 per cent of the diet, and although not rich sources of nutriments, they are available all year round; the animal may spend up to 12 hours a day feeding on the bamboo in order to obtain sufficient nourishment. The giant panda was once classified as belonging to the raccoon family, but has now been placed with the Ursidae (bears). It is immediately recognizable, being large, tailless and appropriately bear-like. It has striking black-and-white fur, offset with huge, dark eye-rings.

Mating starts in March and continues until May, the young being born mainly in August and September. The litter size varies from one to (rarely) three, with twins being quite common. Newborn cubs are blind and helpless at birth and are suckled up to 14 times a day. The young panda opens its eyes

The giant panda is one of the world's most loved and protected animals, and is one of the few whose natural habitat was able to gain a 2006 UNESCO World Heritage Site designation.

at three weeks, but cannot move about independently until it is three to four months old. Weaning lasts for 46 weeks or so. It is a sad fact that even if two or more cubs are born, the mother selects one, leaving the other(s) to die. The surviving cub remains with its mother for about 18 months.

EURASIAN BADGER (*Meles meles*)

The Eurasian badger is found mainly in forested areas and steppes across northern Europe, European Russia, parts of the Middle East, Tibet and China. It is a member of the family Mustelidae, and is therefore related to the stoats, otters, weasels, minks and other badgers. It lives in family groups, establishing territories which include extensive underground burrow systems consisting of tunnels and chambers (known as setts) with several entrances.

Badgers are mainly nocturnal, emerging cautiously from their burrows to search for food. Although members of the order Carnivora, badgers are effectively omnivorous, their diet consisting not only of earthworms, insects, beetles, small mammals, reptiles, amphibians, young birds and eggs, but also berries, roots, nuts, fruits, and other plant matter.

Badgers are playful animals, and their above-ground forays include plenty of romping about, especially by the younger members of the group. Mating normally occurs from late winter to high summer, although implantation is often delayed until conditions are more favorable, with births usually occurring in February or March. Litters consist of between two and six young, although three or four is more usual. The cubs are born blind into the safety of the sett. They open their eyes after about a month, and are nursed by their mother for two and a half months. They may disperse when they are about seven or eight months, although some females never leave, but remain with their parents.

Badgers are popular with the general public, if not with farmers, and societies exist to protect the species. Their most deadly enemy, however, is road traffic.

EURASIAN OTTER (*Lutra lutra*)

The elusive, mainly nocturnal Eurasian otter is one of a family of otters, all of which are highly adapted for an aquatic life. It has a slim body, with a fleshy muscular tail used for propelling the animal through the water. All four feet are webbed, and the nostrils and ears can be closed to prevent water getting in when it is submerged. The animal is found in most of Eurasia and in North Africa, where it frequents rivers, lakes and sheltered coasts. Its main food is fish, but it also takes large amounts of crustaceans such as crabs, amphibians such as frogs, and insects, worms and birds' eggs. The otter builds an underground den in the river bank known as a holt, in which it takes refuge by day. Otters are endearing and playful animals, and there is almost a dog-like quality about them.

The Eurasian otter has a continuous breeding cycle, and mating may take place on land or in the water. Gestation lasts for 60 to 70 days. The female gives birth to two or three cubs, that are born blind. They are weaned for three months and begin to leave the nest after a further two. They soon join

Also known as the European or Old World otter, the animal was celebrated in the famous book, Tarka the Otter: His Joyful Water-Life and Death in the Country of the Two Rivers, *by Henry Williamson, and a 1979 film, based on the book, was also made, narrated by Peter Ustinov.*

in the familiar activities of their kind, such as tobogganing down river banks into the water and chasing after one another – all techniques designed to teach them how to catch prey. The young otters stay with their mother for up to 14 months.

SEA OTTER (*Enhydra lutris*)

The sea otter spends almost its entire life in the sea, a streamlined body, powerful tail, and webbed feet helping it to propel itself effortlessly through the shallow waters of its range, which includes the Bering Sea and the Pacific waters of the California coastline. It likes to frequent kelp forests, where it feeds on a wide variety of marine creatures including sea urchins, crabs, mussels, octopus, squid and fish. Food is grabbed in the forepaws, brought to the surface, and then consumed as the otter lies on its back floating in the water. Difficult items, such as crabs, are broken into by the otter, which rests them on its

The sea otter's primary form of insulation is its exceptionally thick fur coat, the densest in the animal kingdom.

stomach and, holding a rock in its forepaws, uses it to smash the prey open. When sleeping, the sea otter first wraps itself in kelp fronds to prevent itself from drifting out to sea.

Sea otters can reproduce all year round, and females usually give birth once a year after a gestation period that varies from four to 12 months. A single pup is the norm; when twins are born only one can be raised successfully. Females carry out the task or rearing the young. Pups are weaned at about six months on average, but can

begin to eat solid food shortly after birth. To begin with, the pup floats on the surface when the mother is foraging for food. But by two months, the pup is diving for food as well. Mothers teach their pups all there is to know about living in the sea: how to look for food and which foods to eat, how to interact with others of their kind, and so on. The pup usually remains with the mother for about six to eight months. Sea otters are sexually active by about the age of five.

MEERKAT (*Suricata suricatta*)

Meerkats are small carnivores related to mongooses and civets. They are found in South Africa, Botswana, Zambia, Zimbabwe and Mozambique, where they inhabit arid savannah and open plains. Meerkats occupy territory which includes burrows and other shelters and feeding

According to popular African belief (mainly in the Zambian/Zimbabwean region), the meerkat is also known as the sun angel, believed to protect villages from the moon devil or the werewolf, which is thought to attack stray cattle or lone tribesmen.

sites. Highly sociable creatures, they live in packs consisting of up to three family groups, totaling about 30 individuals. There is general harmony within the pack, but fierce battles may erupt between members of rival packs. Co-operation within the pack extends to some members taking turns to keep guard – usually sitting up on their haunches in characteristic fashion – and non-breeding members may look after babies, allowing mothers to forage for food. Food consists mainly of insects and other small creatures, although reptiles and birds are sometimes consumed.

Young are produced throughout the year. Gestation usually lasts for 11 weeks or so, and the mother gives birth to three young on average, born with their ears and eyes closed. They feed on their mother's milk, but need help to urinate and defecate, which the mother provides by licking them to stimulate these functions. The mother picks the babies up in her mouth to carry them about. Males play a part in caring for the young by providing protection. The young are weaned by 50 to 63 days and become sexually mature when they are about a year old.

MOUNTAIN LION (*Puma concolor*)

Also known as the puma or cougar, the mountain lion once ranged widely over North and Central America and parts of South America. Now, however, it is restricted mainly to parts of Canada, the western United States and areas of Central and South America. This large, tawny-colored member of the cat family lives a solitary existence, ranging over a territory as it hunts for deer, rodents and occasionally domestic cattle. It prefers areas such as forest, grassland or swamp with adequate cover and access to plenty of prey, especially if there are caves, crevices and other places in which it can lie up when not hunting.

The territories of male mountain lions often overlap with those of females, and matings occur throughout the year with a concentration from December to March in northern latitudes. Gestation lasts from about 82 to 100 days, with females giving birth every other year. Litter sizes vary from one to six cubs, but three is the average. The cubs open their eyes ten days after birth. At about the same time their ear pinnae unfold, their teeth erupt, and they start to interact with their siblings in play fighting. They are fully weaned by 42 days, but are cared for by the mother until about a year old. The young emit loud chirping calls when they need to summon the mother. Females with dependent cubs use the territory of the father until the young are big enough to move off and establish territories of their own.

In Texas, mountain lions are found throughout the Trans-Pecos and elsewhere, and sightings and kill reports indicate they are occurring in more counties than they did ten years ago, and that they appear to be expanding their range into central Texas.

EURASIAN LYNX (*Lynx lynx*)

The Eurasian lynx is found throughout parts of Europe and Siberia, while closely related species are found in Canada and the northern United States, as well as in Spain and Portugal. These are handsome animals with sturdy bodies, short tails, and distinctive ear-tufts and whiskers. The coat is attractively marked with lines and spots. The Eurasian lynx lives in forested mountainous regions as far away as possible from human habitation, with young lynx spending much of their time in the trees. In winter they do not hibernate but their fur becomes thicker and paler and their large feet serve as 'snowshoes.' The lynx preys on small mammals (such as small deer, hares and squirrels) and ground-dwelling birds, which are either stalked or ambushed. The lynx's keen senses of hearing and sight are used to locate prey.

Mating takes place in spring, with gestation lasting for about 74 days. As birth approaches, the female seeks out a sheltered spot, such as a cave or a hollow tree. The young (usually between one and four kittens are born) are blind at birth and are completely dependent on their mother for warmth, food and protection, with the mother only leaving them when she is desperate for food. The males take no part in caring for the offspring, and with males indulging in multiple matings each year,

Eurasian lynx are capable of producing only short spurts of speed and rely on their hearing and sight to locate their prey. They capture their prey by ambushing them, since they are lacking the endurance for long, drawn-out pursuits.

there is, in any case, no way of knowing which young are their own. Kittens open their eyes at two weeks, and by six weeks begin to accompany the mother on short trips. They are active little creatures, and with their sharp claws they are soon climbing trees. They are nursed by the mother for three to four months, but leave her when they are about a year old and begin to fend for themselves.

LEOPARD (*Panthera pardus*)

One of the 'big cats,' the leopard is a muscular, powerful animal. Its coat is usually tawny or buff with rosette-shaped dark spots, but in some areas all-black varieties occur, known as panthers. The leopard is found in Africa (mainly south of the Sahara but in pockets in the north as well), parts of the Middle East, and in southern Asia. They are at home in a variety of habitats, including forests, swamps, mountainous areas, and grasslands. Graceful and stealthy, leopards conceal themselves well when hunting, which is usually carried out at night. Food includes gazelles, impalas, monkeys, birds, reptiles and even domestic animals such as goats and dogs. Leopards climb well, and when resting will often stretch their bodies out on a high tree branch, balancing by leaving their limbs dangling.

Leopards may mate all year round in some regions, with gestation lasting for between 92 to 112 days. One to three cubs may be born in a den such as a cave, rocky overhang, tree hollow or dense vegetation. Blind at birth, the cubs open their eyes after about ten days. The cubs' fur is longer and grayer than that of the adults, with fewer spots. By about three months the cubs start to accompany their mother on her hunting forays. Weaning takes about 114 to 130 days to complete. By about a year the young are able to find their own food, but they stay with their mother for about 18 months to two years.

The leopard owes its success in the wild to its opportunistic hunting behavior, its adaptability to a variety of habitats, and its ability to move at up to approximately 37mph (60km/h).

CHEETAH (*Acinonyx jubatus*)

One of the fastest of all animals, the cheetah has been recorded at speeds of nearly 70 miles per hour (113km/h). Long legs, a slim muscular body, and a long balancing tail all contribute to this animal's remarkable sprinting ability, made even more spectacular by the way it can change direction in an instant in pursuit of its prey. The cheetah is found in sub-Saharan Africa and Iran, where it favors areas of tall grass within which it can hide as it stalks up close to its victims, which include gazelles, oryx, impalas, rabbits,

birds and young warthogs. The prey is often first located from a lookout point, such as a high rock or a tree.

Cheetahs breed throughout the year, with gestation lasting for about 90 days. Up to eight young can be born, but the usual number is three or four. At birth the cubs are gray in color, and with a mane of hair along the back; this may help conceal them

from predators. For the first few days the mother moves the cubs from place to place to confuse predators while she is away hunting. Mortality is high, however, with lions taking many cheetah cubs. At about six weeks of age the cubs are sufficiently well-developed to follow their mother around. Weaning is completed in a span of from 120 to 150 days.

Adaptations that enable the cheetah to run as fast as it does include large nostrils for increased oxygen intake, and a large heart and lungs that work together to circulate oxygen efficiently. During a chase, its respiratory rate increases from 60 to 150 per minute. The cheetah also uses its tail as a rudder-like means of steering, to allow it to make sharp turns to outflank its prey.

LION (*Panthera leo*)

The second largest of the big cats after the tiger, the lion is a muscular animal with a tawny coat and a thin, black-tipped tail. Males have shaggy manes, and are the only cats to have such a feature. Cubs have brown spots on a grayish coat until they are about three months old. Most lions live in sub-Saharan Africa, where they favor

Lions have been kept in menageries since Roman times and have been sought after and exhibited in zoos the world over since the late-18th century. Today, zoos are cooperating worldwide in breeding programs for the endangered Asiatic subspecies.

savannah and bush country. The once wide-ranging Asiatic lions are now confined to the Gir Forest in north-west India. Lions

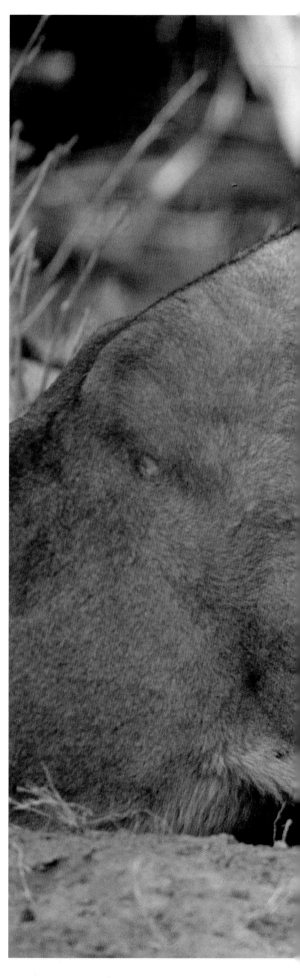

congregate together in groups known as prides, which may consist of up to 40 individuals, but most are much smaller at around a dozen or so animals. Several males, usually brothers, rule the pride, the rest of which comprises related females, including daughters. Within the pride there is considerable co-operation in activities such as sharing the suckling of youngsters, and in food capture.

The lionesses are the hunters for their pride and capture their prey by means of precise and complex teamwork. Males are less effective at bringing down prey (which in Africa includes zebras, wildebeest, buffaloes, impala and giraffes), but they nevertheless claim dominance when it comes to feeding on the kill.

Lions breed all through the year, with a three- to four-month gestation period. One to six cubs are born, which open their eyes when they are about 11 days old. They are able to walk by about 15 days and can run at about a month. Infanticide is quite common among lion prides, and the mother keeps the cubs hidden until they are about eight weeks old. Weaning may go on until the cubs are ten months old, but they are dependent on other adults in the pride until they reach the age of at least 16 months. Males do not care directly for the cubs, but their presence is important in protecting the young from rival males. They also seem to show a remarkable tolerance toward young cubs, letting them bite them and clamber over them in play.

JAGUAR (*Panthera onca*)

Ranging from the south-western United States down to Argentina, the jaguar is a large, solidly-built big cat. It is similar to the leopard, although the jaguar is stockier and has a larger head. It is found in a variety of habitats, including jungle and scrub. Jaguars are solitary animals, roaming their territory and looking for prey, which includes deer and peccaries. In habitats where there is water, jaguars frequently catch fish, turtles and small alligators, being able to climb and swim well.

Jaguars are sexually mature at three years of age. Gestation lasts for 93 to 110 days, after which time the female gives birth to one to four cubs in a secure den among rocks or in dense vegetation. Cubs are blind

Because of their reclusive nature and relative scarcity, due to habitat loss and poaching, little is known of jaguar behavior in the wild. What is known comes from studying them in captivity.

at birth and do not leave the den for two weeks, and are weaned after about 180 days. They learn to hunt at six months, but stay with the mother for up to two years.

TIGER (*Panthera tigris*)

The largest of all the cats, at around 13ft (4m) in total length and weighing up to 660lbs (300kg), the larger tiger subspecies are comparable in size to the largest extinct felids. With their orange-red coats, with vertical black stripes along the flanks and shoulders, and white underside, tigers are instantly recognizable, although there are several variations including almost totally white individuals with brown stripes.

Tigers are among the world's charismatic megafauna, featuring in ancient mythology and folklore, and appearing on flags and coats-of-arms, as sporting mascots, and as the national animal of several Asian nations.

The tiger's once-huge Asian range is now reduced to parts of Korea, China, Russia and India, where it occupies a variety of habitats such as forests, scrub, and mangrove swamps, and can tolerate a wide range of temperatures from hot, tropical conditions to well below freezing.

For most of the time tigers are solitary animals, active both day and night as they stalk their prey through dense vegetation, where their striped bodies provide excellent camouflage. They can also climb and swim well. Prey consists of animals such as deer, water buffalo, bears, leopards, crocodiles, rats and turtles.

Tigers may breed at any time of year, but November to April is the most common period. After a gestation of around 100 days, the female gives birth to one to seven helpless, blind cubs, whose eyes do not open until they are six to 14 days old, the mother staying with her offspring during this dangerous period. The cubs begin to accompany their mother on hunting trips when they are about two months old, at which time they begin to take solid food, although they are weaned for a period of 90 to 100 days. The cubs start to play an active part in hunting trips when they are about six months old, learning from their mother how to stalk, catch and then kill prey; play fighting between siblings also helps to develop these skills. The cubs remain with their mother until they are 18 months to three years old, after which they disperse to set up their own territories.

SNOW LEOPARD (*Panthera uncia*)

The snow leopard, or ounce, is a rare and elusive animal that inhabits the mountains of central Asia, favoring alpine steppes and coniferous forest, but which is also found in places such as the Gobi Desert. It has thick soft fur and a long bushy tail, used as a counterbalance when jumping and to wrap around the body when the animal is at rest. Cream or smoky-gray above, the lower parts of the body are white, the coat often lightening in winter. The pelt is marked with dark spots, rings or rosettes, and the head with round black spots. The ears are small and very

Snow leopards are well-adapted to their environment, their large feet acting as snowshoes and their legs having been designed for jumping, with hind legs longer than the fore. Large nasal cavities allow them to utilize the oxygen in the thin, cold and dry air of high altitudes to the maximum.

furry – an adaptation against the cold – as are the animal's large paws, which also help it get a grip in the snow. Sheep, marmots, hares, mice and deer form the bulk of the diet, but livestock is also taken on occasions.

Usually solitary, the snow leopards may share a range when mating, which occurs between December and March, followed by a gestation of 100 days. One to five young are born in a rocky den that the mother lines with her fur to keep them warm. The young are blind for the first nine days, after which they open their eyes. They leave the den to follow their mother around when they are three months old, but are dependent on her for about a year. They are weaned at between 50 and 180 days.

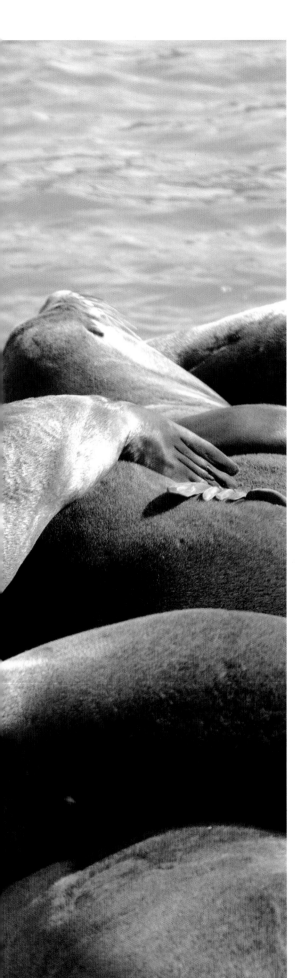

CALIFORNIA SEA LION
(*Zalophus californianus*)

This sea mammal was once popular in circuses, and it is still a favorite in zoos and marine theme parks. The California sea lion mainly lives in groups along North America's western coast, but also around the Galapagos Islands, where it swims and dives capably for fish and squid using its powerful flippers. It may also come ashore to bask on jetties, piers and beaches.

In the breeding season, which peaks in July, males claim territories on remote beaches and islands for several weeks. Gestation lasts for about 11 months, with a

On warm days the sea lions remain close to the water's edge, but move inland or up coastal slopes at night or on cool days. Outside the breeding season, they often gather at marinas and wharves, which provide a degree of safety from their natural enemies, the orcas and white sharks.

single dark-coated pup usually being born in May or June. At birth, the pups are already capable of swimming, and can move about on land within an hour or so. The mother weans the pup for about six months to a year. She uses scent to help locate her offspring among the many similar-looking baby seals in the group.

COMMON SEAL (*Phoca vitulina*)

The common, or harbor, seal is the most widespread of all the pinnipeds (the group that comprises the seals and the walrus), being found in temperate to Arctic waters on both sides of the North Atlantic and North Pacific Oceans. Common seals are usually solitary animals, apart from when they are mating, rearing young, or when they haul out with others of their kind to bask on beaches and sandbanks. These communal gatherings, however, are still essentially solitary affairs, with most individuals reacting angrily if another approaches too closely. The common seal feeds on shellfish, squid, and fish.

Common seals are brown, tan, or gray, with distinctive V-shaped nostrils. Adults can achieve a length of 6.1ft (1.86m) and a weight of 290lbs (131.5kg).

Mating generally takes place from spring through to fall and is carried out in the water. It is preceded by play activity in which males and females grab each other's necks and blow bubbles. The gestation period is around nine to 11 months, with a single, woolly-coated pup usually being born, which can swim from birth and can dive in the water when only a few days old. Weaning lasts for about three weeks, after which the pup is left to fend for itself.

GRAY SEAL (*Halichoerus grypus*)

Found in temperate and subarctic waters on both sides of the North Atlantic Ocean, the gray seal may be seen hauled out on rocky coasts, isolated islands or ice floes. Fish, squid and crustaceans form the bulk of the diet, usually eaten under water and swallowed whole. This is a social feeder, with several individuals gathering together to feed when there are rich pickings. The male gray seal has a long head and snout, giving rise to its nickname of 'horsehead.'

The breeding season varies according to different populations, but may be any time between December to the following October. Breeding grounds, or rookeries, form on beaches, islands and ice floes. Both sexes feed avidly before breeding; for the female, this is because she will need to feed her pup on stored food reserves once it is

In the United States, gray seals are typically found in large numbers all along the eatern coast of North America up to the coastal waters of New Jersey, off New England states, and slightly less frequently in the mid-Atlantic states, although its natural range extends to Virginia.

born. Gestation lasts for 11 months, and a single pup is usually born. Newly-born pups have long, creamy-colored fur which is replaced after about three weeks. Pups are nursed and weaned for about two weeks after birth, with the female proving an attentive and protective mother. Once the pup is weaned, the female mates again and leaves the pup to fend for itself. It remains on land living off its fat reserves until it molts again, at which time it enters the sea to feed. Young gray seals may disperse for many hundreds of miles from the place where they were born.

ASIAN ELEPHANT (*Elephas maximus*)

Widely domesticated, the Asian elephant has been used in forestry for centuries, moving logs, also for religious and ceremonial purposes.

The smaller of the two elephant species, and identified by its smaller ears, more humped back and the single projection on the tip of its trunk, the Asian elephant is nevertheless an impressive and powerful creature and one of the two largest land animals, standing 10ft (3m) at the shoulder. Found in parts of India and South-East Asia, the Asian elephant's habitat includes scrub forest as well as deeper jungle, where it browses a wide variety of vegetation including grasses, bark, roots, stems and leaves. The vegetation is grasped in the trunk before being transferred to the mouth.

These are social animals, and a herd usually consists of an old female together with about 20 or so of her younger female relatives and sometimes a male as well. Males often travel alone or in loose all-male groups. The hottest part of the day is spent resting in the shade, the animals' large ears helping to dissipate heat from their bodies.

Usually only dominant males mate with females. Breeding takes place throughout the year, with females giving birth every three or four years. Gestation lasts for 18 to 22 months, and a single calf is born, which is able to stand up shortly after birth. At birth a baby Asian elephant may weigh up to 220lbs (100kg). The young elephant starts to eat grass a few days after birth, but continues to be weaned for up to four years. It also eats its mother's dung, which contains nutrients and also bacteria useful for digesting the cellulose present in plants. The young elephant continues to be supervised by its mother for a couple of years after weaning, and keeps close to her as the herd roams about in search of food.

AFRICAN ELEPHANT
(*Loxodonta africana*)

The imposing African elephant is the world's largest land animal, with a fully grown bull (male) standing about 12ft (3.75m) at the shoulder. African elephants are distinguished from their Asian relatives by the former's longer ears and tusks and by the fact that it has two finger-like projections on the tip of its trunk. African elephants once roamed widely across sub-Saharan Africa, but today, through a combination of habitat destruction, hunting and illegal poaching, they are chiefly confined to a few wildlife reserves in southern Africa.

Active day and night, African elephants wander the savannah, arid regions and forests, often in herds of up to 200 strong, even more on occasions, feeding on leaves, roots, fruits, shoots and sometimes crops. The elephant society is matriarchal, the leader being an old female which leads a group of a dozen or so subordinate individuals, consisting of related females and their young. Once they have reached maturity, males tend to become solitary or wander in groups made up of other males.

Once the time for mating arrives, males indulge in displays of dominance that include head-shaking, trumpeting, ear- and trunk-raising and head-swaying. Gestation lasts for 22 months, after which time usually a single calf is born, weighing in at about 265lbs (120kg). Within a short period, the young elephant is able to follow its mother around – a necessity to avoid the

African elephants ingest large amounts of vegetation, which is defecated without being fully digested. This, combined with the long distances covered daily in search of food, contributes to the dispersion and germination of numerous plant seeds.

vulnerable animal falling prey to lions and other predators while it is still small and helpless. The calf is suckled for at least two years, but may remain with its mother for considerably longer – all of her life in the case of a female. While it is growing, other females in the herd – sometimes including its own older siblings from previous matings – help to protect and care for the youngster, which includes suckling it from time to time. Sexual maturity is reached by the age of ten or 12 years.

PLAINS ZEBRA (*Equus burchelli*)

The plains zebra is found mainly on savannahs and plains in east and southern Africa, where it roams in small groups consisting of a male, his harem of females, and their young. Sometimes several such groups join together to form large herds. The black-and-white body patterning of zebras is well-adapted to confuse predators. When groups of zebras are standing together, the patterning breaks up the animals' outlines, making it hard for lions and other predators to pick out individual victims to attack. Zebras are active by day, and spend their time roaming the grasslands and waterholes.

Foals may be born at any time of the year, although the peak is during the December to January rainy season. Gestation lasts for 370 days and a single foal is produced. Newborn zebras can stand within a quarter of an hour of being born and begin to suckle their mother's milk within an hour. For the first few days the mother drives away other members of the group if they come too close, but following this period the foal begins to interact with the rest of the group. Mothers are very vigorous in defence of

The quagga was the first extinct creature to have its DNA studied, and genetic research at the Smithsonian Institution has demonstrated that it was in fact not a separate species at all, but diverged from the extremely variable plains zebra, Equus burchelli, *between 120,000 and 290,000 years ago, suggesting it should be named* Equus burchelli quagga.

their young, biting and kicking at would-be predators, although the sad fact is that many young zebra fall prey to lions, hyenas and other such enemies. The foal is suckled for about a year.

WHITE RHINOCEROS
(*Ceratotherium simum*)

With their distinctive nose horns, stocky, armored bodies, and reputation for charging, head-down, at aggressors, rhinoceroses are one of the best-known of all the African 'big game' animals. At 13ft (4m) in length, the white, or square-lipped, rhinoceros is the largest of several rhino species. Now endangered through years of indiscriminate hunting and poaching, this animal is restricted to game reserves in parts of southern and north-east Africa, where it grazes grass and other vegetation. Females tend to gather in small groups with other females and their young, but males tend to be solitary.

White rhinos mate throughout the year, with peaks occurring in summer and autumn. Gestation lasts for about 16 months, and a single calf is born which is able to walk soon after birth. As with many large, herbivorous animals of the open plains, the ability to become mobile without delay is vital in the struggle to

*There are two subspecies of white rhino, with South Africa having the greater share of the first, the southern white rhino (*Ceratotherium simum simum*), this being the most abundant. It will readily breed in captivity if the conditions are right.*

avoid being eaten by predators. Weaning takes one to two years, during which time the calf stays with its mother. At about two to three years, the mother is ready to mate again and the calf is driven off to begin a life on its own.

WILD BOAR (*Sus scrofa*)

Ranging across parts of Europe, Africa and Asia, from Siberia down to South-East Asia, the wild boar has a broad distribution and is found in forests and open woodland. The animal's heavy body is covered with bristly hair, and males have prominent tusks. Wild boar live in small groups of about 20, consisting of females and their young. Males live alone, but often in quite close proximity. Active at any time of the day or night, wild boar forage for bulbs, roots and nuts, at other times lying up in dense vegetation.

The tusks of the males come into their own in the mating season, for they are used as stabbing weapons in fights to decide the

BABY ANIMALS

After whitetail deer, wild boar are the most popular introduced game animal in the US, where they are called razorbacks, pineywoods rooters, feral boar, and Russian or European boar.

right to mate with females. The young are born after a gestation period of between 100 and 140 days, and litters consist of anything from one to 12 or so offspring. The nest is a grassy structure, deep in cover, and the piglets remain in it, feeding from their mother's teats for about ten days. When young, the piglets have striped fur, as this patterning gives them camouflage among the foliage. Weaning lasts for about four months, and the young are independent by about seven months.

HIPPOPOTAMUS

(*Hippopotamus amphibius*)

The huge hippopotamus is superbly adapted for a life spent mostly in rivers and lakes. It can swim and dive well – and can even run along the bottom – and its feet have webbing between the toes. The hippo occurs in the Nile river valley in East Africa, having been annihilated from much of its former sub-Saharan range. The animal spends most of the day in the water, floating almost submerged, with just its eyes, ears and nostrils visible. By night it may sometimes move ashore to rest and graze vegetation. Groups of about 30 or so

animals may be seen together, centered around females and their offspring. Females are vigorously fought over by males at breeding time.

Hippos may breed all year round, but there are peaks during February and August. Gestation lasts for about 230 to 240 days, and a single calf is born, the birth being timed to coincide with the period of most luxuriant waterside plant growth. Suckling lasts about a year, and the calf is often nursed under the water. As the calf grows, it often rides on its mother's back in the water for safety.

The hippo's skin secretes a natural, red-colored sunscreen substance, sometimes referred to as 'blood sweat,' although it is neither blood nor sweat. The secretion is initially colorless and within minutes turns red, eventually turning brown.

FALLOW DEER (*Dama dama*)

The fallow deer's natural range includes southern Europe, Asia Minor and North Africa, but it has also been widely introduced to many other places, including North and South America, Australia and New Zealand. This deer can tolerate varied conditions, including scrub and subalpine vegetation, although the preferred habitat is temperate deciduous broad-leaved woodland with grassy clearings. Male fallow deer have large, flattish palmate antlers. Males and females have coats with white spots, although the coat is quite variable, being white or even black in some individuals.

In the northern hemisphere the rutting season is between September and January. Bucks (males) defend territories and round up does (females) for mating. Gestation lasts for 33 to 35 weeks, after which a single fawn is born, usually in a secluded spot that the mother has already selected for the purpose. The mother immediately licks the fawn clean, establishing the important mother-baby bond. The fawn is kept by the mother in its hiding place, and it lies there quietly until she returns to nurse it – which happens at regular intervals throughout the

Fallow deer have been introduced into some areas of central Georgia where, being without natural enemies, they have greatly multiplied, causing serious damage to young trees. They have also been introduced into Texas, along with many other exotic deer species, where they are kept on large game ranches.

day. Weaning continues until the fawn is about seven months old. After about three weeks the mother and her fawn rejoin the herd of other females and their young. The young become independent at about a year.

222

GIRAFFE (*Giraffa camelopardalis*)

The tallest of all the animals, the stately giraffe stands nearly 17ft (5.3m) tall. This great height, the result of both its long legs and its very long neck, means that it can browse the tops of the tallest trees that other herbivorous animals cannot reach. This is an evolutionary mechanism to ensure that similar browsing herbivores do not all compete for the same food. The giraffe inhabits savannah country and open woodland south of the African Sahara. Giraffe are social animals, living in herds, or troops, of six to a dozen individuals comprising females and their offspring and a male.

Mating takes place in the rainy season, with usually a single calf being born from May to August during the dry spell after a 455-day gestation. The mother gives birth standing up, and so the newborn calf must endure a 6-ft (2-m) drop to the ground. After this somewhat brusque start to life,

the calf gets to its feet and is able to suckle within 15 minutes. The mother conceals the young giraffe on the ground for the first week or so of its life, although she remains close by and returns to feed it at night. After a couple of weeks the calf becomes part of a crèche, overseen by other mothers in the troop. This enables individual mothers to go off and feed and rest themselves before returning to suckle their calf at night.

Weaning takes 12 to 16 months. Young female giraffes stay with the herd, but when young males become independent they leave the herd to obtain one of their own by ousting the incumbent male. Females become sexually mature at three or four years, and males at four or five years,

Unfortunately, young giraffe can fall prey to lions, leopards, spotted hyenas, and wild dogs, although their characteristic patterning possibly provides a certain degree of camouflage. Even so, only 25–50 per cent reach maturity.

although they may not breed for another couple of years.

AMERICAN BISON (*Bison bison*)

Once, millions of bison roamed the North American plains, but they were brought almost to the point of extinction through hunting by settlers. However, vigorous conservation programs have meant that their numbers have recovered somewhat, and small semi-wild herds are again seen in places such as the western United States and Canada's Northwest Territory. The American bison is a huge,

American bison are often called buffalo, which is technically incorrect as they are not true buffalo. The bison group comprises the American bison and the European bison or wisent, a related group of wild bovines, more closely related to cattle and yaks.

impressive grazing animal, with a humped back and shaggy fur covering the head, shoulders and fore legs.

The breeding season begins in June and finishes in September. After a gestation period of about 285 days, a single calf is born in thick cover away from the main herd. The young calf has fur of a reddish color, which starts to turn brown after a few months. The calf can walk and run within a few hours of birth, and stays close to its mother. The mother cares for the calf for about a year, by which time it is fully weaned. Males do not participate in the care of the young.

MOUNTAIN GOAT
(*Oreamnos americanus*)

The mountain goat, also known as the Rocky Mountain goat, is a distinctive-looking animal with a thick white coat and beard and black horns, the large oval horns being specially adapted for gripping rocky surfaces. Its natural range is Alaska, western Montana and Idaho, but it has also been introduced into areas such as South Dakota. It prefers steep, rocky areas with cliffs up to about 8,000ft (2438m), migrating from high elevations down to lower regions during winter.

Courtship begins in September, and breeding starts around November.

BABY ANIMALS

Gestation lasts for about 160 days and one to three young, known as kids, are born. Birth usually takes place on steep, inaccessible cliffs so that predators cannot get to the young. The young are mobile soon after birth and are weaned after about three or four months. They need to be agile from an early age, and are soon able to move around among the crags. The kids also practise climbing techniques by clambering onto their parents' backs. After weaning, kids usually remain with their mother until she gives birth to further young.

In lower regions, below the treeline, female mountain goats will protect themselves and their offspring by fighting off predators, such as wolves, wolverines, cougars, lynx and bears. But very young kids are in constant danger of being taken by golden eagles.

EURASIAN RED SQUIRREL
(*Sciurus vulgaris*)

The range of the Eurasian red squirrel comprises the forests of Europe and northern Asia. In Britain, however, where it was once widely distributed, it is no longer found in any great numbers, its place having been taken by the introduced gray squirrel (*Sciurus carolinensis*), an American species. The red squirrel lives and builds its nests in both deciduous and coniferous forests, with seeds, pine cones and acorns forming the bulk of its diet. Any excess food is stored in tree cavities or is buried in the ground.

The red squirrel builds a spherical nest, called a drey, with a framework of twigs and a lining of moss and grass. Each squirrel may use several dreys. Like the gray squirrel, red squirrels do not hibernate, but will remain in their dreys for days at a time in bad weather. Mating takes place between January and March, and the litter may consist of one to eight young (usually three), following a gestation period of 36–42 days. The young are born blind and hairless. They open their eyes at about 30

Although red squirrels usually remember they have laid down caches of food, their spatial memory is substantially less accurate than that of gray squirrels, and they will often have to search for these hiding places with the result that many such caches are never found again.

days and leave the nest for the first time after about 45 days. They are weaned at seven to ten weeks, and are independent by 16 weeks. Only the female looks after the young. Two litters may be produced in a year when conditions are favorable.

GRAY SQUIRREL (*Sciurus carolinensis*)

The gray squirrel's original natural range was the eastern United States and parts of Canada. But introductions mean that it is now found in the western United States as well as in places such as Great Britain. In this latter region, the gray squirrel has usurped the native red squirrel in most areas. The gray squirrel prefers deciduous forest, such as oak, but it is found in other types of forest including coniferous. Food includes fruits, nuts, seeds, insects and birds' eggs. Like its cousin the red squirrel, the gray squirrel is adapted to a life in the trees, and is an acrobatic climber and jumper, its bushy tail helping it to maintain balance.

Beginning in spring, two litters are produced each year, after a gestation period of 44 days. Each litter consists of two to four young (sometimes up to eight), and

Gray squirrels, when they are still young, don't yet know instinctively what is good to eat, and therefore sample all kinds of random things, discarding them broken and half-eaten.

the newly-born young are blind and naked. They are cared for in the nest, or drey, until they become independent, having been weaned for up to ten weeks.

EASTERN CHIPMUNK
(*Tamias striatus*)

This bold and curious little rodent is found in most of eastern North America, also in Minnesota, Wisconsin, Iowa, Illinois and Michigan, and in southeastern Canada. Eastern chipmunks build shallow burrows under the ground, often beneath logs and boulders, which can be up to 30ft (9m) in length and can consist of

Eastern chipmunks prefer habitats where there are abundant crevices in which they can take refuge, along with elevated observation and vocalization points. They can also be found in urban and suburban areas, where they make their homes in yards and beneath porches.

several different tunnels. There are also various entrances and exits, covered with leaves and rocks to avoid detection by

predators. A wide variety of food is consumed, including nuts, seeds, fruits, birds' eggs and insects. The name chipmunk comes from the 'chip chip' noise these animals frequently make.

Females produce two litters per year, each after a gestation period of about 31 days. Litters usually number four or five, but up to nine young have been known. The young are born into the safety of the underground burrow, where they are cared for by their mother, not emerging above ground until they are six weeks old, after which they begin to disperse. Sexual maturity is reached at about a year old.

EURASIAN BEAVER (*Castor fiber*)

Like its American cousin, the Eurasian beaver is one of nature's great engineers, felling trees by gnawing through them with its sharp, chisel-like incisor teeth so that it can construct a dam in a river or lake. The animal then builds its home, called a lodge, in the resulting pond it has created. The beaver is the second largest rodent, after the capybara, and is well-equipped for its semi-aquatic lifestyle, having a flattened spade-like tail used for swimming, webbed feet, dense insulating fur, and nostrils and ears that it can close off when beneath the water. Food consists of all kinds of vegetation, including twigs and bark.

Beavers breed once a year, during January and February, after a gestation period of 105 days. Litter sizes usually vary from one to three youngsters. At birth, the

The European beaver is an endangered species, having been hunted almost to extinction in Europe, both for its fur and for castoreum, a secretion used for scent-marking, and believed to have medicinal properties.

young have a full coat of fur and open eyes. Weaning takes about three months, but the babies can take small amounts of other food items after a few weeks. The young are confined to the lodge for the first week or so, but they then venture into the water for the first time. Beavers live in family groups, consisting of the male and female parents, newborn young, and juveniles from recent years' matings. Parents and juveniles all help look after and feed the very youngest members of the family. Year-old beavers can, at this stage, help in family activities such as dam-building. They normally distance themselves from the family when they are about two years old.

HARVEST MOUSE
(*Micromys minutus*)

This is a tiny, attractive rodent, only 4.5in (11cm) long. It is found in Europe east to the Urals, where it favors arable farmland, hedgerows and reedbeds, wherever there are places it can build its spherical, plaited breeding nest, which is about 4in (10cm) across. Smaller non-breeding nests are about half this size and are built closer to the ground than those for breeding, which tend to be positioned well up in vegetation to help avoid predators and flooding. The harvest mouse is an extremely agile climber, using its prehensile tail to grip corn stalks and other vegetation. A variety of seeds, insects and fungi form the main diet, some of which is hidden in underground caches against hard times.

Breeding lasts from May to October, and up to seven young are born in each

The harvest mice is Europe's smallest rodent, and is the only Old World mammal to have a truly prehensile tail.

litter, with three litters normally produced each year. The tiny young are born into the breeding nest, where they are suckled by their mother for 15 days or so. After that time she abandons them, and the young may remain in the nest for a few more days before dispersing.

HOUSE MOUSE (*Mus musculus*)

One of the most common of all rodents, this animal is not only found in houses and other man-made structures, but is also encountered on waste ground and in hedgerows. The house mouse originated in Asia, but it has spread all over the world, and probably vies with the brown rat for the title of the most widespread of all wild mammals. The keys to its success are its adaptability, in that it can live almost anywhere and eat almost anything, and its fast breeding-rate.

The female house mouse produces between five and ten litters per year, each of which consists of four to eight young. They are born into nests hidden away in quiet spots and lined with whatever soft materials

House mice usually walk and run on all fours, but stand up on their hind legs when eating, fighting or orienting themselves.

are available. In houses this may be wood shavings, chewed-up paper, and fragments of cloth. Babies are suckled for three weeks, after which time they are on their own.

SNOWSHOE HARE

(*Lepus americanus*)

Found in forests and thickets throughout Canada, also in Alaska and some western and eastern parts of the United States, the snowshoe hare has a dark-brown coat in summer, which changes to white in winter, apart from black edging on the ear-tips, the winter coat helping to disguise the animal in the snow. The animal has heavily furred hind feet with wide-spread toes, and these help it move easily through the snow. It has quite small ears, compared with other hares, and this smaller size helps to reduce heat loss. Active by night and in the early morning, the animal feeds on shoots, grass and buds.

The snowshoe hare's breeding season starts around mid-March, with the first of several litters being born in May after a 36-day gestation period. Litters range in size from one to 13 young, the number born increasing as the season progresses. The youngsters are born with their eyes open, being fully-furred and able to hop about almost immediately. They are

The snowshoe hare, also known as the varying hare, gets its name from the fact that the animal's hind feet are very long and the toes can be spread out to act like snowshoes, preventing it from sinking into the snow. These large feet also have fur on their soles, which protects them from the cold and increases traction.

suckled once a day by their mother, usually in the evening, and in between times lie quietly in a depression or out of sight of predators. They are independent when they are about four weeks old.

RABBIT (*Oryctolagus cuniculus*)

The ancestor of the domestic rabbit, this species was originally confined to the Iberian Peninsula and parts of France, but introductions throughout history have seen it spread to places such as Australia and South America. Rabbits prefer grassland with cover nearby, and are often seen near downland, woodland edges,

A rabbit's hind feet have a thick padding of fur to dampen the shock and facilitate quick movement. Its toes are long, and are webbed to keep them from spreading apart as the animal hops.

roadside verges and sand dunes. The rabbit builds an extensive underground burrow system, known as a warren, into which it quickly retreats at the first sign of danger; several hundred rabbits may occupy a large warren. Rabbits are mainly nocturnal, leaving the safety of the burrow to graze on vegetation and crops at night, although when feeling it to be safe, they can also be active by day.

Mating occurs throughout the year, but most litters are born between February and August. Litter sizes can range from three to ten or so young, produced after a pregnancy of between 28 and 34 days. The young, or kittens, are naked, blind and helpless at birth, and are born into a special burrow lined with vegetation and fur plucked from the mother's belly. After about a week, their fur starts to become visible, and after a few more days their eyes have opened, followed by their ear openings. The outer ears, tiny at birth, now also start to grow rapidly. The kittens stay in the burrow for three weeks, during which time they are fed on their mother's milk. When she leaves the nest, the mother (doe) carefully conceals the entrance to avoid predators spotting it. The young are weaned after 28 days.

GLOSSARY OF TERMS

Adult

Fully mature individual capable of breeding.

Brood

A group of baby animals produced or hatched at one time. It also refers to the activity by which a parent keeps its eggs or young warm.

Calf

A term used to describe the young of several different types of mammals, such as cattle, elephants and whales.

Chick

A young or recently hatched bird.

Clutch

The eggs laid in a single breeding attempt.

Crèche

A gathering of young animals which are often temporarily looked after by other members of their group.

Cub

A term used to describe the young of several different types of mammals, including those of foxes, bears, lions, tigers and cheetahs.

Den

A natural or constructed shelter used for sleeping in or for giving birth to and raising, young.

Egg tooth

A small, sharp projection that develops on the bill of a chick while it is in the egg. The chick uses the egg tooth to cut its way out of the shell. The egg tooth is later absorbed.

Embryo

Early stage in the life of an animal while it is inside the egg or its mother's womb.

Fawn

A young deer.

Fledging

The period at which a bird grows its flight feathers and is ready to fly.

Foal

A young member of the horse family.

Gestation

The time an animal spends developing inside its mother; pregnancy.

Hatch

To break out from an egg.

Holt

The nest of an otter.

Implantation

The point at which the early embryo becomes attached to the wall of the mother's uterus.

Incubation

The process during which a fertilized egg develops ready for hatching.

Joey

A young kangaroo, wallaby, or possum.

Juvenile

An animal that no longer has infant characteristics but is not yet fully adult.

Kitten

A term used to describe the young of several different types of mammals, including domestic cats.

Litter

The offspring of a single pregnancy.

Mammary glands

A milk-producing glands found in most mammals.

Marsupial

A type of mammal, whose young are born at an early stage of life and then continue their development in the mother's pouch, or marsupium, which contains the mammary glands.

Nest

A place specifically for the rearing of an animal's offspring. Nests range from simple holes or scrapes to elaborate, purpose-built structures.

Nestling

A young bird in the nest.

Pup

A term used to describe the young of several different types of mammals, including dogs, seals and sharks.

Scrape

A rudimentary kind of nest made by forming a depression in the ground and typical of some kinds of birds.

Siblings

An animal's brothers and sisters.

Suckle

To feed on the mother's milk provided by her teats.

Territory

An area that an animal considers its own, defends, and habitually uses for breeding.

Weaning

Transferring from a diet of the mother's milk to an alternative, usually solid, source of food.

Yolk sac

A small sac containing yolk that hangs from the under surface of some animals, especially certain types of fish, and which provides them with nutrition for a period of time.

INDEX

ACKNOWLEDGEMENTS

All images including the front cover supplied by: © Heather Angel/Natural Visions Photo Library www.naturalvisions.co.uk other than the following:

Back cover; Flickr Creative Commons/Seth M.

©iStockPhoto/Alain Turgeon; page 224 left. Anders Tomberg; page 138. Andrew Howe; page 235 right. Art G; page 194 left. Betsy Dupuis; page 251. Britta Kasholm-Tengre; page 219 below. Bruce McQueen; page 240. Chanyut Sribua-rawa; page 169. Christoph Ermel; page 218. David P Lewis; page 242. David T Gomez; pages 141, 200. David Warshaw; page 183 right. Dieter Spears; page 247 above. Frank Heung; page 203 above. Gertjan Hooijer; page 245 above. Graeme Purdy; page 223. Henk Bentlage; page 163. Hilton Kotze; page 186 left. Jason Pacheco; pages 182 left, 192. Jim Kruger; page 148. Jonathan Heger; page 180-181. Karol Broz; pages 177, 179. Kelly Zunker; page 249. Ken Channing; page 203. Klaas Lingbeek-van Kranen; page 243 right. Geoff Kuchera; page 175. Kurt Hahn; page 219 above. Laurie Neisn; page 238. Megen Lorenz; page 178 left. Nancy Nehring; page 201. Pauline Mills; page 222. John Pitcher; page 176. Paul Reid; page 241 below. Peter Malsbury; page 168 above. Rainforest Australia; page 99. Ralt Broskvar; page 239. Rick Wylie; page 233. Rotofrank; page 234. Thomas Pickard; page 139 below. Tina_Rencelj; page171 right. Chanyut Sribua-rawd; page 196. Wayne Pillinger; page 168 below.

National Park Service; page 246.

Flickr Creative Commons/: Alison McKeller; page 22. Alun Salt; page 54. Anita Martinez; pages 48 above, 49. Bartdubelaar; page 120 above. Beatrice Murch; page 173, 175 right. Ben Cooper; page 55. Benedict-Adam; page 57. Bill Dolak; page 71 below. BingoBangoGringo; page 82 above. Brell Marlow; page 33. Casey Brown; page 229. Chad Miller; page 39. Chester200; pages 114 below left, 118 above. Chris Barber; page 244. Claus Rebler; page 56 above. Corrie Barlimore; page 37. Cowboy Dave; page 35. Crackers93; page 82 below. Dan Gordon; page 90. Dave-F; page 83. Dave Pape; pages 195 right, 197. David Cook Wildlife Photography; page 93. David Dennis; pages 100, 214 left. Dennis Wright; page 24 below. Eddie Callaway; page 152. Eddy van 3000; page 245 below. Ed Schipul; page 117 below. Eric Bégin; page 74 below. Frank Wouters; page 220. Gina Pina; page 19. Harlequeen; page 151 above. I Love Trees; page 109. James Emery; page 26 above. Janice Milnerwood; page 166 left. Jan Kalab; page 62 left. Jason Steffens; page 52. Jeff Kubina; page 151 below. Jennifer Slot; page 226 below. Jim Bowen; pages 117 above, 146. Jim Champion; pages 23, 24 above, 25, 26 below, 27, 32 above. Joachim Humber; page 104. Johan Dreo; page 31. John Haslam; pages 80, 81 both. Jpmatth; pages 74 above, 75. Kaitlin Means; page 227. Katrinket; pages 50 above, 56 below. Keven Law; page 127. Kimberley; page 230 above. Kyrill Poole; page 71 above. Laszlo Ilyes; page 44. Laurence; page 70. Lauri Rantala; page 50 below. Lee Coursey; page 241 above. Leni Rachael; pages 187 right, 187 right. Lisa Yarost; page 225 right. Marieke Knijpers; page 122 below. Markus; page 212. Mathias Erhart; page 43. Matt Musselman; page 48 below. Matts Lindh; page 94. Maurice Koop; pages 29 below, 36. Michael 'Mike' Baird, bairdsphotos.com: pages 132, 133, 134, 164, 165, 167 right, 202 above. Michelle Tribe; page 73 right. Mike Willis; page 231. Millie; pages 2, 28. Monica R; page 84. Mountain Amoeba; pages 30 above, 230. Niels; page 53. Niki Odolphie; pages 125 right, 128, 129. Old Banb; page 32 below. Oli R; page 96 above. Pattycakes 1108: page 139 above. Paul Pod; page 77 left. Photon-de; page 51. Pieter Lanser; pages 40, 41, 42. Pete D; page 98. Peter Békési; page 47. Rabesphoto; page 149. Ralph Daily; page 226 above. Red Jar; page 34. Richard Fisher; page 45. Richie Graham; page 30 below. Rob Chandler; page 88. Robert Eugberg; pages 188 left, 190. Rosemary; page 216. Ryan E Poplin; page 121. Scott Chalon; page 123. Sebastian Bergman; page 86 right. Seth M; page 69. Sharon Mollerus; page 21 right. Shiny Things; page 119. Sir Merus; page 118 below. Steve and Gemman Copley; page 202 below. Stevie-B; page 77 right. Stig Nygaard; page 107 right. Stuart Chapman; page 207 right. Tambako the Jaguar; pages 102 left, 108, 126, 184 both, 185, 191, 193, 198, 199, 221, 228. Tashiya Mirando; page 114 above. The GirlsNY; page 89. The Repairman; page 97 below. Tiny Froglet; page 86 left. Tobias; page 29 above. Tony Harrison; page 38. Tony Hisgett; page 76. Twinkle Lettkeman; page 18. Z Pics; page 120 below.

Wikimedia Commons/: Andreas Trepte; page 204 left. Bob Tomasso; page 147. Dave Pape; page 162. Fir0002; page 92. Gibe; page 97 above. Hinke/Sacilotto, Alaska Maritime National Wildlife Refuge. Lars Karlsson; page 96 below. Leyo; page 95. Ray Eye; page 232.